# Exp(
# Mastery

## How to use digital marketing to turn your expertise and experience into high-paying customers.

## James Nicholson

# Expert Mastery

First published in the United Kingdom in 2017 by James Nicholson.

Copyright © James Nicholson 2020.

James Nicholson has asserted his right under the Copyright, Designs and Patent Act 1988 to be identified as the author of this work.

ISBN-9798612708186

# ACKNOWLEDGEMENTS

Writing a book involves a huge number of people.

Although they may not be directly involved in the researching, writing and editing process of the book, their influence and advice over the years I have been studying and implementing marketing has undoubtedly rubbed off on me. This book is the culmination of all the education, training, strategy sessions, workshops, interviews, phone calls, critiques and hushed conversations I've had the benefit to be a part of.

There are almost too many marketers to mention who have been part of my journey, some simply as a source of information, others I have directly worked with. I have always believed that if you're the smartest person in the room, you're in the wrong room and so I have worked hard to seek out people to learn from who were at the top of their game. Their ideas and helps have shaped my ideas and helped me give birth to concepts and strategies which I'm sharing with you.

Where I have used another's idea to demonstrate an argument or highlight a point, I will make a point of giving credit. In many ways, I know I'm standing on the shoulders of giants, but hopefully with this book I can help you and other marketers stand a little bit taller and see a little bit further.

The cast of individuals in this game are many and I would like to thank those who have particularly inspired me, including Frank Kern, Dan Kennedy, Ryan Deiss, Russell Brunson, Andy Harrington, Jessen James & Jody Raynsford.

I'm sure I've missed out a ton of people who I'll slap my forehead remembering once this book has gone to print, so I'll add thank you to everyone who has been part of my journey so far.

I would like to thank my team, without whom none of this would be possible. We work hard to keep the wheels turning and they're good at letting me fly with ideas, while making sure my feet end up rooted back on the ground. If there's one thing, my team and I are good at, it's implementation. So thanks team - we did it!

I'd also like to thank…

My friends and family who have stood by me in the good times and the bad, believing in my crazy ideas or at least allowing me to follow my dream without much protesting while I risked everything on numerous occasions.

And a special mention to my good friend Graham Dymond, who tried in vain to talk me out of writing this book!

Graham this one's for you mate, I hope you enjoy this every Christmas for the rest of your life.

# TABLE OF CONTENTS

# CAN THIS BOOK HELP YOU?

If you've not heard of me before and you're picking up this book to have a quick skim before buying, let me give you the lowdown.

My name is James Nicholson and I'm an expert in digital marketing. I have helped thousands of businesses take their expertise and turn it into customers.

I could tell you about the millions of pounds myself and my agency has spent running advertising across Google, Facebook and Youtube. But that wouldn't mean much to you.

What you probably care most about right now is sales and getting customers. Without doubt, that's what most people need to ease the challenges they may be facing. Ultimately, you want something more. To be in charge of your own destiny. To have control over your life so you can gain the freedom to do what you want, when you want. More sales and customers are just the means by which you can get to that point.

Now, getting you more customers may seem like a big promise. I mean, there's a 101 scammy marketing pros out there who will promise the earth and deliver nothing.

They'll tell you this doesn't work so you now need to try it this way. Or, they'll explain everything has changed and what you're doing is wrong. If you're like me, you can see right through their cheap tricks.

But you now have an advantage... you know someone who actually practises what he preaches. And it's my goal to be of service to you.

You'll be shocked to realise the majority of people who sell training that promises to make you "famous" in your field or deliver a "flood of leads" don't actually do half the things they say YOU need to do.

You may also be surprised to hear that getting this right isn't *actually* that hard. It's in the interests of these "educators" to persuade you that you can't do this, that you need their help. Nothing could be further from the truth. You can do this... you just need to know what to do.

(I should know. I wasn't taught by anyone. Everything I know, I learned for myself over 10 years of good, bad and ugly courses... and, of course, spending a fair few pounds on advertising).

## Here's why I wrote this book:

To show you how to use the system I developed over many years to position yourself as "The Expert" and attract customers to you without being "salesy" or sleazy.

That's what you'll find in the next 200 or so pages.

What you won't find are cheap tricks or tactics that may win a few sales here and there, but ultimately damage your brand and reputation in the long-run.

I'm guessing you're reading this book because you want a change. You want to get from where you are now to somewhere else that has eluded you until now - whether that is doubling or tripling your income, having more free time, making an impact or simply fulfilling your potential.

If that's right, then I would like you to make a promise - not to me - but to yourself.

You see, I can share with you all the strategies and secrets I've spent years perfecting and using to help my clients make millions. Yet there's one BIG "secret" to enjoying enduring success that almost no-one talks about. And it's the sole reason why people succeed or fail.

It's not about how clever you are, or how much training you've done. It's nothing to do with the amount of money you have to invest in advertising, nor on the contacts you have or the size of your current audience.

The "secret" is much more powerful than that. And I attribute this to my own success.

It is the ability to IMPLEMENT what you have learnt.

I have trained thousands of people in what I'm showing you here in this book. That doesn't mean thousands of people have become rich, famous, or closer to whatever their life and wealth goals are. Because this one element separates them... the ability to implement.

For many years, I gave presentations where I showed this system to a hundred people at a time. And I'll catch up with some of those people a few weeks later to find out what they have done.

Two people in the same room, learning the same knowledge *should* get the same results. Yet, again and again I see people rising far above everyone else simply because they've taken the time and effort to implement the free information I've given them.

In fact, I've seen businesses double in size on the back of the information I share for free. And I've heard the same excuses from individuals who listened to the same information and still didn't do anything with it, even though it was clearly in their interest.

I want you to be one of the former. The successful ones, who use the knowledge they learn and change their life as a result.

So, that's why I'm asking you to make a promise now. Promise yourself you will read this book and take action.

It doesn't matter how small or how imperfect, just take action.

Because taking any kind of action will allow you to start to build momentum. When you start building momentum, you see results. And those results will compound and compound again and again as you fly forward towards achieving the income, freedom and impact you always wanted.

Make that promise and let's get started.

# INTRODUCTION
## (OR WHY YOU SHOULD LISTEN TO ME...)

I never wanted to be an expert. And I never wanted to be a marketer. I thought my career path was going to be very different.

To say that I fell into both of these positions is an understatement. I more tripped, stumbled and flew through the air towards where I am now. Along the way, I've taken some varied paths and experienced some real highs and lows, from being £50,000 in personal debt up to running a business turning over £2 million a year. Until I ended up where you see me today.

There was one thing I knew I wanted right from being a young child.

I knew I wanted to be rich.

I never wanted to worry about money ever again. Because when I was growing up, there was never *any* money. And the really sad part of it was that money wasn't our family's biggest worry.

My home wasn't the best environment for any child. My mother suffered from mental illness and was an alcoholic. Because my mum was incapable of doing anything, our house was - to put it mildly - a shithole. And because of her addiction we never had any money.

As a child, you live with what you know, but even then I knew we were poor. We couldn't afford a school uniform and I had the embarrassment in going into school everyday with a uniform pieced together from hand-me-downs or borrowed from others. I didn't get presents at

Christmas. It was horrible. If you have children, imagine what it would be like not having the money to be able to treat them once a year. Imagine how they would feel when they saw everyone else receiving presents only to find they had nothing to open on Christmas morning.

It doesn't bear thinking about. There is good news from this. The experience made me clear at young age what I wanted. I decided that I didn't want to live like that any more.

So I did something about it. When I was 10, I used to go out car washing in the neighbourhood to earn a few pounds or I would go looking to do odd jobs. I even went carol singing at Christmas - although to this day I'm unsure whether people gave generously because they enjoyed my warbling to them or wanted me to stop! And then on my 16th birthday, I moved out.

I lived in a rented room in someone's house and found a job at the local Burger King. Driven by my desire to earn as much money as I could, within a year I had become the manager of the store. At 17, I was officially the youngest Burger King manager in the whole of the UK. Quickly, though, I realised my opportunities for progression were limited.

At this point I moved into recruitment sales working in the IT sector. Now, I wasn't the greatest sales person ever. In fact, I would describe myself as average back then. It was hard, really hard. You see, in recruitment, you needed to sell twice - once to the employer and once again to the potential employee. But the money was good.

With the spoils of my employment, I decided to go backpacking for three months, which then turned into twelve months. I had such a great time. I travelled all over Asia, then to Australia and New Zealand. It was here that I had an epiphany which led me to start my first business.

In Thailand, it was normal for backpackers to buy cheap, knock-off CDs from vendors along the Khao San Road in Bangkok. With a CD player in tow, you could carry around 20 or 30 CDs to play while enjoying the sights of South East Asia.

But one day, I was sitting next to a guy on a boat who pulled out of his backpack an iPod. I'd never seen an iPod before and like some wide-eyed child seeing something incredible for the first time I told him, "That's amazing!".

No prizes for guessing what the very first thing I bought was when I got home was: an iPod. I started back with the recruitment company again but now I had a plan. I'd seen something called the iSkin, which was a silicone case you could put on the iPod to protect it.

I wondered to myself, "what if *I* could sell these?". I took the initiative and contacted a wholesaler in the UK who stocked them and bought a batch for the grand sum of £50. With my first batch of stock, I set about building an eBay business selling the cases online.

This was my first taste of being an entrepreneur, and I quickly had to learn how to get good at selling on eBay.

You never forget the first time you make a sale online. I remember my first eBay sale as though it was yesterday. It was bizarre - almost mind-bending - to think that somebody who I had never met and who I had never spoken to was buying my product. They had handed over their cash and I had made my first profit. It was a real buzz. And I was hooked.

Fast forward six months and things had escalated quite dramatically.

## Growing an online business

Because I was still working at the recruitment firm, all my deliveries had to come to the office. These deliveries started off small but eventually the size and number of boxes increased to a point where there was quite a bit of grumbling. The company were generally pretty good about it, as they wanted me to stay working there. But one night, once everyone had gone home, I had to spend several hours driving back and forth in my car transporting 30 boxes. I then had to spend pretty much all night packing and shipping to customers. Something had to give.

I was at a crossroads.

Do I keep it small or do I jump in and make this into a proper business? Although it felt like a big decision at the time, looking back now there was never really any doubt.

I took the leap and started working on turning my little eBay venture into a full-time business.

I started with getting my own office. It was just a tiny, little space in Dorking town centre where I lived. Little did I realise it would soon become the headquarters of a million pound business!

Most businesses who start up usually take a few years or so to get into their stride before hiring any staff. Just two weeks after setting up in the office, I hired my first full time member of staff.

Getting your first employee is always rather special. For me, his name was very memorable - Lee Boggis. He helped out with everything at that time and soon our tiny office was heaving with stock. As we sold stock, we bought even more in and my business grew and grew.

Then someone happened that shook me. Just weeks after I started working in the business full-time, the 7/7 bombings took place in London. If you were around when this shocking event happened, it rocked the country. Everyone was stunned this type of terrorism was back on our streets after everything that happened with the IRA back in the 1980s.

"What a time to start a business," I thought, as all those thoughts of self-doubt and worry flooded through my mind. If you're an entrepreneur or business owner, you'll know exactly how it feels. Those first few weeks, months or even year when you're still unsure whether you've made the right decision or not.

Not that any of my friends and family were any help. None of them could understand why I left my easy job in recruitment sales, where I was making decent money... to sell these silly little accessories on my own.

## Why you're part of the top 1%

I guess if you've never been an entrepreneur you never understand how it feels. The majority of people seek the security of a wage. They can't understand why you would leave behind a decent wage, holiday pay, benefits and perks... to spend even longer working for less pay (for the moment, at least), more responsibility and more worry.

I'm also guessing that you and I have a pretty similar outlook - otherwise you wouldn't be reading this book - and we understand all those worries and concerns are worth it for the freedom and independence.

We understand that to create a life we want to live, we first have to make sacrifices and do things we don't necessarily want to do (and that 99.9% of people wouldn't never dream of doing).

But at this point, this dream of freedom and huge amounts of money in my bank account and success was a long, long way away.

At this point in my business, I was knee-deep in boxes, juggling money so I could pay suppliers as quickly as I could make sales and trying to manage a growing team.

It's amazing whose paths you cross in your life and who goes onto stuff you can't believe when you see it.

One day a young guy came into my office looking for a job. So I hired him. He worked for me for a bit and we spent a lot of time chatting in the office, normally talking about our interests. The subject got onto sport and I distinctly remember having a chat with him about rugby. He told me he used to play rugby and he wasn't that interested in it any more and that he preferred other sports. Now that doesn't sound that interesting until I tell you who this young lad was... George Kruis.

Yes, THAT George Kruis who now plays for the England rugby team.

If that wasn't a lesson that your past doesn't define your future, I don't know what is.

## Journey into digital marketing

The company was doing well and we had hit £1 million in revenue but I wanted faster growth. Faster, much faster growth than we were experiencing.

I needed more customers coming to our website and buying. I needed more traffic.

We were using an SEO company in Ireland who we paid to sort out our keywords and do what was needed to drive new customers to the site organically.

But I wanted them to do more - and, of course, I was more than willing to pay as I knew this was a positive long-term investment. The problem was the SEO company couldn't handle it.

Seriously! Despite my offers to pay them more money to do more SEO, they didn't have the capacity to work on my business even more. The reason was we had become too big

and if we became more than half of their total business, they would be in a precarious position.

It makes sense from a business point of view... but ultimately it was very short-sighted on their part as it forced me to become good at SEO myself and I eventually pulled all our business from them.

So, how did I get good at SEO?

Attend an expensive 12 week training plan to set myself up for SEO success?

Find a mentor and pay them thousands to teach me all their secrets?

Well, not quite. I bought a copy of *SEO For Dummies* and started there. Yes, I invested a measly £10 in a book that gave me the starting points for building what became an essential marketing asset for my business. Although I added some more advanced courses to my education after that, all my success in SEO started with that £10 book.

The important thing to remember - as you'll discover throughout this book - is it's not about the information.

You can find information on how to do anything EVERYWHERE. It's not information we lack. It's something even more basic.

The ability to TAKE ACTION.

What made me different from everyone else who bought that book and didn't successfully generate a ton of free traffic from SEO? Well, it wasn't brains because I didn't know a thing until I picked up the book.

It was simply this. I read the book and put everything I learned into action.

And if you want any better reason why you should do the same to everything I share with you in this book, it's this.

That £10 book helped me go on and turn a £1 million turnover business into a £2 million turnover business within a year.

Then everything fell apart...

**Losing everything**

I can remember the exact date it happened... 12 July 2009.

I was sitting at my office staring at my screen at some of the sales reports from the previous month. In that moment, I was feeling delighted that we were experiencing strong month-on-month sales growth. We hit £2 million in sales and the business was only getting bigger.

If you've ever owned a business for any amount of time you'll know the rollercoaster effect. That experience of feeling happy one moment and then desperately low the next. This was one of those moments.

While I was sitting at my desk, one of my team members came rushing through the door to speak to me. As I looked up at them, I instantly knew something was very, very wrong. They told me the worst news I could've possibly heard:

We had been banned from selling on Amazon.

As we were selling online, a high proportion of our sales were going through Amazon.

The Amazon marketplace was one of the areas where small businesses could very rapidly grow using Amazon's infrastructure. The only problem was payments would go via Amazon which meant every time you sold something they would collect the money and give it to you a few weeks later. With a business our size and the number of transactions we did each day, that amount was high. As a fast-moving business we relied upon those payments coming through like clockwork, every week.

Although it was a £2 million a year revenue business, our margins were tight. There was more competition now and we had to squeeze everything we could from our process. Cash flow was one of my biggest concerns. This meant I had to be super-careful with my income and expenses. There wasn't any room for error or we'd end up going under.

Now I'd just been told Amazon had closed our account with £55,000 of our money still to be paid to us. Overnight, my business ground to a halt.

The worst part was this is all come about because I tried to do the right thing.

When you sell on Amazon, the most important part of your marketing is getting good reviews and lots of them. Even just a few negative reviews will push you behind your competition.

From all the positive reviews, we received one negative review from a customer who made a complaint. It wasn't about our service but about the product they bought, which was slightly different to what they expected.

As you can imagine, for an online retail business there are always a lot of refunds. Products appear differently to how people's expectations are when they buy. It's just something online retailers have to deal with.

In this instance, the individual did not make a complaint to us first or ask for a refund. Instead, they immediately posted a negative Amazon review.

In trying to resolve this, I contacted them and said I would happily refund them and send them a new product.

And if I did that would they be happy to change their review?

I thought this was gonna make the situation better. However, it (technically) fell foul of Amazon as it could be considered a "bribe" - and in many senses, it was. This individual immediately complained about it to Amazon and Amazon Banned us from selling on their platform.

Because of this one person my business was destroyed.

Due to Amazon holding £55,000 of our funds things became impossible to manage, we struggled to pay our bills on time. Suppliers cut our credit lines, some of which were over £1,000,000. Our cash flow was in a crisis and it became impossible to continue to trade, within a few months the business had to close.

I literally had to close a £2 million business because I could not trade. I had lost everything.

I could've walked away from the business owing thousands to suppliers and staff. However, I've worked with a lot of great people over the years and so I wanted to make sure everyone was paid up, despite the fact I could have run away from my responsibilities - as so many businesses do. I didn't want to ruin all the relationships I had, even though I may never work with any of those people again. That's just the person I want to be.

Now that may sound stupid or naive. That may be different to how many others would advise. But that is how I want to operate.

As a result, I ended up with £50,000 in personal debt.

It was a huge bump for me. Going from running a £2 million business which was successful - although not hugely profitable - to now being in a situation where I had worse than nothing. I now had to figure out how to get out of a huge amount of personal debt.

## A new low

As a child, I vowed I would never again be in a situation where I had no money. That was precisely the situation I found myself in when this happened. In the months after, I slipped into depression.

I struggled to get out of bed. I stopped seeing friends and stopped speaking to my family.

It was easy for me to shut myself off.

But it wasn't the worst of it.

If you've ever been in a huge amount of debt you'll know how anxious you become. You're constantly worried the next knock on the door is a debt collector or someone coming to take the last of what you have.

You know what it's like to have to pretend that you're not in when you hear that knock. Or to be scared every time the phone rings. That's exactly how I felt.

It was a period that made me sad and frustrated because I thought I'd left all this behind.

But from the ashes of defeat, there was another opportunity for me. This opportunity was doing for others what I had done for my own business - creating digital marketing campaigns that generated customers and sales.

And that was how I became the UK's leading digital marketing expert...

## From the ashes to a leading expert

Despite growing a business and then watching it collapse, it took this crazy journey to discover where my true value lied. That's when I had an epiphany:

I was a digital marketing expert.

I had a particular set of skills that were incredibly valuable to a huge number of businesses.

And I could do the ONE thing so many businesses struggle with: find new customers to bring in sales and make higher profits for the business.

It wasn't until I hit that new low that it uncovered my true value and from then it was clear I needed to promote myself as THE digital marketing expert.

Not only was I an expert in growing businesses online, I discovered how few other experts were out there. There were so few people with real-world expertise and experience building an online business from scratch it was shocking. Everywhere was flooded with so much misinformation about what it took to win new customers in this new online landscape.

I also realised that there was a huge opportunity for businesses, freelancers and consultants who were insightful enough to make the jump to using digital marketing and use this to grow their income.

This was 7 years ago and I still believe we haven't even reached the limits of the opportunity out there.

I started an agency back then called SEO desk, offering - surprise, surprise - SEO for businesses. This morphed into a full digital marketing agency and I worked with some of the biggest businesses and brands in the country, including the NHS, to generate traffic for them and drive more customers and more sales into their business.

**Our first exhibition stand at The Business Show in Earls Court**

After my success with the agency, more and more business owners and entrepreneurs sought me out to help them with growing their business through digital marketing.

I simply didn't have the time, but I saw a chance to educate and help a huge number of people. That is why I set up The Business Accelerator - a community of switched-on business people who are ambitious for growth and take action to get more customers and more sales.

After reading my story, you may be sat thinking,

"That's all great James, but how does that help me?".

I began this book talking about how you can transform where you are now to where you want to be. And, in telling you my journey, it wasn't my aim to move you to tears with a sob story or gain sympathy.

It's simply to show you that...

- ❖ no matter what your situation
- ❖ no matter the amount of debt you may currently have or the challenges you face
- ❖ no matter how tech savvy you are or how little you believe you can do this
- ❖ no matter how far you think you are away from being seen as an expert, respected, looked up to and paid well for your expertise
- ❖ no matter how far away your ideal income, your dream home and the freedom to do what you want and when...
- ❖ it IS possible.

I know because I'm living proof. And what's more, I've helped thousands of business owners, freelancers, coaches, consultants and many, many other professionals design the life they want and achieve it for themselves.

In a moment, I'll share with you the exact steps you need to take to get there. But first, there are some beliefs and myths you may be holding onto which we need to smash before we go any further.

# THE FORMULA FOR SUCCESS

Getting paid what you're worth and having the freedom to live the life you want to lead is possible.

Forget that. It's not just possible, it's EASY... when you know how.

Many of the business experts or gurus out there want you to believe it isn't easy. They *need* for you to believe it's hard. When you believe it's hard, it's so much easier for them to tell you their programme or their training is the key to getting what you want. They have a vested interested in making you feel like you need to jump through hoops to get whatever it is that you want.

They're lying to you.

The formula success is really very simple. So simple, it's shocking.

I know this because I have worked with some of the biggest entrepreneurs in the UK and across the world. I've been in high level mastermind groups and consulted with them. And I've learnt a lot about what it is that separates what they do from everyone else.

I'll share this with you in a moment.

But, first, let me tell you what doesn't make a difference.

... you DON'T have to have huge amounts of money to invest or have huge resources at your disposal

... you DON'T have to be the most knowledgeable person in your industry, even to become known as THE expert

... you DON'T need to have a huge existing network in place and rely on referrals for business

... you DON'T need a super big profile to start out with to gain the attention that you need.

And you certainly DON'T need to pay thousands and thousands of pounds to so-called business or marketing coaches who you've never heard of and never actually do half the things they teach to get started.

You just need to understand THREE simple things to start moving in the right direction.

Knowing these puts you a long way ahead of most people in your industry who still believe the misinformation peddled to them.

When you know these elements, you will be able to take what you learn in this book and make serious steps towards living the life you want to live, making the income you've always wanted and enjoying all the freedom you wish.

What are the three things?

These three things taken together are nothing short of a success formula. And the first element is exactly what you need to consider to become the "go to" person in your sector.

## 1. Positioning

The first thing you need to do in order to gain more money, more attention and more better clients than anyone else in your sector is to be positioned better than everyone else in your market.

What do I mean by "positioning"?

Positioning is about how your audience perceives you. It's about how they see you compared with other people in your market. How do you rate how well you're perceived as an expert in your industry? Are you even seen as an expert compared with others providing a similar service or offering a similar product in your industry?

One easy way to think about positioning is in terms of the car industry.

A Volkswagen is positioned as a more premium version than a Skoda. Yet for many of those vehicles they share the same chassis, the same engine and many of the same features. There is one major difference - one has a VW badge and the other a Skoda badge.

What allows a manufacturer to charge almost double the amount for a VW than for the Skoda?

Positioning.

It's all about perception.

Let me ask you another question: is Tony Robbins the best life coach in the world?

Think about that for a moment.

Sure, he's the *highest paid* life coach in the world. And, sure, he's the *best-known* life coach in the world. But is he the BEST life coach?

Probably not. There are probably MANY people out there who are better life coaches than Tony Robbins. They may be better but they're not earning anywhere near what he's earning - currently around $1 million per private client. They're not gaining the kudos nor respect he receives. They're not playing to packed out conference rooms and venues where people pay up to $15,000 to see Tony in action.

And the reason is nothing to do with Tony's ability as a coach.

It's EVERYTHING to do with his positioning. He knew how to position himself as the world's best life coach.

Getting your positioning right is key to everything you want to achieve in your life. Follow Tony Robbins' model.

Before we work on this, it's important to know something else. While it takes concerted effort to position yourself well in your industry, it's very easy to do the opposite and "de-position" yourself.

I see so many people do it all the time.

It's easy to de-position yourself by...

- ❖ offering your services for lower than you're worth
- ❖ begging for business
- ❖ being far too accessible to everyone regardless of whether they are your ideal customer

This is a mistake I used to make before I understood what was needed to position myself as an expert. Here's the crazy thing. I can guarantee you don't LIKE to do any of those things - not a single one - that de-positions you in the eyes of your target market. Here's what to do... don't do it any more. Seriously, make the commitment right here to not beg for business, sell yourself short or be at the beck-and-call of your customers.

Draw a line in the sand today and say "NO MORE". And live it.

Let me also make it clear. You don't automatically get positioned as an expert by virtue of just being really good at what you do. It doesn't work like that. You have to engineer your positioning to get the result you want.

And to do that you need this next element...

## 2. Visibility

The second most important trait to have success is visibility.

What you need to know about about positioning is that half the battle is making sure you are seen. Every time, ALL the time.

As I explain later in this book when I reveal the strategies of Expert Mastery, what Internet gurus and so-called online marketing "pros" tell you about what you should do is often very different from the reality.

I know because I've sold enough products and services, and helped enough businesses within my agency and now as an internet marketing teacher and coach, to know what works and what doesn't. My clients tried a lot of the "strategies" suggested by the gurus and they all came away frustrated, disappointed and were still stuck.

I don't pull any punches. It doesn't make me popular with many business owners who are happy to keep their head in the sand… but it's devastatingly effective when working closely with businesses who want to make a killing online and build an incredible expert business that supports their lifestyle. I tell them what I know works and what doesn't.

If you think you can get away with being invisible and dreaming you're suddenly going to achieve widespread profile, acclaim and recognition with some hack or secret, you're going to be a lot more than sorely disappointed.

You're going to be poor. For a very long time.

Even if you could select your target clients and contact them directly, it still wouldn't provide you with a consistent reliable system through which to generate and leads and sales and grow your expert business. Being seen all the time is key to everything in this system.

What needs to happen is this:

Your positioning must be communicated to your audience in the most visible way possible. You must be seen as demonstrating all the elements of your expertise across the most important channels to market.

If that sounds like a whole ton of hassle, let me tell you now - it really isn't. All you need is a well thought-out strategy and a clear plan for achieving maximum visibility on a long-term basis and deliver your value as an expert to the right audience at the right time.

You can certainly waste time, effort and money if you throw mud at the wall and hope something sticks.

That's what most businesses do when getting their message "out there". They try anything they can and it's painful to watch, and they inevitably fail. Usually, they're trying the same tactics they've always tried and hoping for a better result - despite the fact that most of those tactics have long lost their effectiveness.

This may mean putting out an advert in a local newspaper or magazine. Or sinking a ton of cash into a radio campaign. Or leafleting their local area. Or getting up at 5am, putting on a suit and pitching to a room of less-than-perfect business owners who are more interested in eating their free breakfast.

The old ways of reaching your audience no longer work. It makes me cringe when I hear people still paying PR firms to do the usual dance of trying to secure "free" publicity in the form of reviews, articles and news stories. Or bringing an intern in to "do social media" for their business and knocking out a stream of terrible cliches and quotes on pretty backgrounds that will somehow magically manifest itself in new leads and customers.

Let me let you into a not-so-little secret: these won't position you in the right way to bring you the leads, customers and profits you need to achieve the income goals you've set yourself or grow your expert business.

Predictability and measurability are two important drivers behind getting your face in front of the people who matter: your buyers. And mastering digital marketing will allow you to do that in a timely and predictable way.

Of course, I *would* say that.

My background is in digital marketing. I know its power and its effectiveness, and how quickly you can utilise something that works to scale up your income and your growth.

Great positioning needs to go hand in hand with a mechanism by which you can get yourself in front of your audience in the right way at the right time and do it either for free or at profit. No other marketing form will deliver a positive, measurable return on investment as quickly when you follow the right system. And no other marketing or publicity method will give you the freedom and independence - so much of this process can be automated or outsourced once you get to a certain level.

But we're jumping ahead of ourselves now and this is covered in more detail later in this book. I will show you exactly what to do and how to do it in order to get the visibility you need to become a highly-paid, recognised expert in your area.

And that brings me onto the third part of the success formula…

## 3. Consistency

The third most important trait is obvious but also at the same time the hardest to achieve. Consistency in your approach is how you beat all your competition and dominate your market.

It's that simple.

Keep going and going and going and going.

The best part is, using the principles of business growth and the tools of digital marketing, you will eventually arrive at a point where your systems are perpetuating your activity and you don't need to grind it out.

But grinding it out at the beginning is what you may have to do. Because there is one major obstacle to achieve truly powerful consistency in your sector. And this one is hugely problematic.

Because it's YOU.

You are the engine of the system I'm about to show you how to create (at least at the beginning). That means you need to be working with the system for long enough until the system starts to gain traction and you can put other elements in place to take the weight off you.

As you'll see when I show you the Expert Mastery strategies, there is good news. Being consistent isn't onerous. In fact, it *should* be simple. You're not going to be asked to do anything you can't already handle or learn new skills or try something completely outside your sphere.

You are going to be doing the things you are good at: being an expert in your field, speaking to your audience and showing the world what you're capable of.

The only thing that WILL hold you back is your commitment to taking consistent action to work on both your positioning and your visibility. Regardless of whether client work gets in the way, or you have limited time in your schedule for other commitments, you need to commit to showing up.

Show up on a regular basis for your audience and you'll succeed.

Seriously, so few people do it, you'll stand out.

Also, I can't promise you that this won't take you out of your comfort zone or expose you to some fear about your ability to deliver. You may even think you're a fraud at times or get nervous about "imposter syndrome" simply because you're going to be putting yourself in front of more people than you ever have.

This is perfectly normal. I'll help you get through it. You just need to trust in the process and believe me when I tell you that EVERYONE who has successfully built an expert business has gone through exactly the same shifts.

One of the best ways to power through self-doubt, worry and confusing is to commit to being consistent and showing up every day with your ultimate goal in mind.

Are you ready? Great, let's get started.

Now you've seen the three parts of the formula for success and know what you need to be aiming for, there's another little ingredient we need to throw into the pot to help you push past those feelings we just talked about.

And it may just be the most powerful force you've ever trained on your career...

# THE POWER OF YOUR WHY

WARNING: When you go through this system and move towards Expert Mastery, you're going to experience feelings you may have felt before... but perhaps more intensely than you've ever experienced.

As alluded to above, you need a powerful driving force behind you that's going to kick you up the arse every time that voice in your head tries to talk you down from taking action. It needs to be something urgent enough to make you leap out of bed every morning raring to go. It needs to stop you procrastinating for hours on ends making an important sales call or recording a short video you know your audience wants.

You need to know your "WHY".

Everyone needs a WHY. Your WHY is the reason you're doing all this, the reason you're going outside of your comfort zone and laying it all on the line. It's the reason you're putting yourself up for potential ridicule, abuse and, ultimately, possible humiliation when it all goes wrong.

Your WHY gets you through all these. You just need to work out what it is NOW before we continue.

Here's my WHY:

Everything I do in my business is because of my family. I keep this image close to me at all times and it helps me when I'm struggling over a decision, or feel fear rising up in me when I'm about to do something big for the first time.

Yours may also be your family. But then it may not. It could be your friends, your community, a cause that's really important to you… I can't tell you what your WHY should be. Only you know that.

But you have to become crystal clear on that WHY and you really need to feel it and believe it.

This is only a short chapter, but it only needs to be. We're bringing attention to whatever is already inside of you, but drawing it out to use as a tool in our campaign to turn you into a highly paid expert.

I want you to take a few minutes to think about your WHY. Who is it? What is it?

When you've taken the time to think about it and get it down on paper or saved to your computer or phone, put it to one side yet never forget it.

Time now to roll the sleeves up and look at the 11 strategies of Expert Mastery and how they can help you…

# THE 11 STRATEGIES OF EXPERT MASTERY

In everything I teach and everything I advise the businesses who we work with and my private Inner Circle clients, I have one rule I stick to.

Everything I share with you comes from experience. I do not - and will not - suggest anything in relation to growing or marketing your business that I have not tested, tried or implemented myself.

This is what people tell me sets me apart from the hundreds of Facebook celebrity internet marketers who are vying for the attention of business owners and entrepreneurs. I'm a practitioner.

I implement the exact strategies and systems I show you in my own business. I know they work.

I also know how these systems work when other entrepreneurs and experts use these in their own business. I know they work.

In short, they work. To fully appreciate why some systems work better than others, there are a number of strategies which are important to understand. You probably know a few of these already.

Seriously, I don't claim to be teaching anything particularly ground-breaking. It's the combination of strategies within one system of marketing that really makes a system work.

With you - and your expertise, knowledge and value - at the heart of this marketing system, you have the opportunity to build the business of your dreams.

Understand and then implement these 11 strategies and you'll not only gain Expert Mastery, you'll smash your income goals, enjoy more freedom and independence and change more lives and have a greater impact than you ever thought possible.

And right at the heart of the first strategy is YOU…

# STRATEGY #1
# YOU, THE PERSONALITY

Even in the world of digital marketing some things never change.

The one thing that gets our attention and keeps us reading watching or listening are stories about people. As humans we are hardwired to be interested in other humans. Human emotion and human stories are what drives the biggest online and news publications in the world.

Seeing how other human beings act and interact with each other keeps us captivated, whether we like it or not. We are walking, talking, gossiping, nosey, emotionally-driven beings who are psychologically primed to be interested in one another.

No amount of new technology or new ways of communicating with each other will ever change that.

Technology has amplified this even more than before. When we go to social media platforms, such as Facebook, Instagram Twitter, or Pinterest we have the opportunity of sharing our stories as well as diving into the stories of others and creating our very own real life soap operas.

There is a lot going on psychologically behind this and discovering more about our fellow human being also has a physiological element. A chemical in our brain called dopamine is released every time we see a new piece of information. It is highly addictive. It's released every time something catches our attention. And what gets our attention more than anything else? Other people.

You'd be forgiven for thinking I'm trying to pitch myself a an editor of a sleazy tabloid or a gossip site.

What I'm trying to communicate is that to gain attention online and to gain visibility for yourself with your audience, you need to tap into this important trait of human behaviour.

This is true whether you're digital marketer, a PR, a traditional advertising exec, a speaker, a politician or anyone else in the public eye.

You have to captivate your audience. Then, you need to hold their attention.

Fortunately, while this sounds well beyond what you may expect to have to do in order to grow your business (and may seem to cross the boundary between personal and business life), it really isn't any much more work than running a

marketing campaign. You just need to know how to cleverly use the tools at your disposal to have the most effect.

It's all about working smarter rather than harder.

**Business Video Tip I Created While Quad Biking In Cambodia.**

Here's how we do this.

What if I told you that right now there is no excuse for not finding your way in front of your audience? The most important thing is to know exactly where your audience hangs out and put yourself in front of it. Very few buyers will not be on a platform like Facebook, so Facebook is a great place to start.

In the past, when you wanted greater visibility and wanted to put yourself in front of your audience the plan was to call the media sales team of a national newspaper and spend £5,000 to put a one-off ad in the publication and hope for results. Or spend £20,000 for a TV spot, then an additional £10,000 on its production and wait weeks for it to air.

Those days are long gone. You can now put yourself in front of a global audience within minutes using the social media platforms and technologies available to you for FREE. That's why it makes sense to understand who your audience is so you can more closely target them and most social media are you to do this simply.

Not only can you gain global reach, you do not pay a penny for access to YouTube, Facebook or any other social platforms your audience resides on. If you do decide to go down the paid traffic route – and that is something we'll discuss in this book – you can gain even greater reach than most other businesses.

## Put yourself out there

You are surrounded by opportunity. But this opportunity means nothing if you don't take advantage of it.

One of the most valuable decisions I ever made was to commit to putting myself out there as much as possible in as many ways as possible. Whether it's through images, video or audio content, getting myself in front of and gaining the attention of my target audience has been the most powerful driver of success for my business.

And, yes, I have managed to achieve this without paying a penny to do so when building an audience.

However, before you think "wow, that sounds easy" I need to be brutally honest with you.

Most people don't enjoy the success that I have enjoyed. Most people don't come close to reaching the number of people I reach. Most people and most businesses don't get anywhere near the amount of visibility of exposure I achieve. And there's a good reason for that.

Most businesses, coaches or consultants will simply not put in the time or effort it takes to put themselves in front of their audience on a consistent basis.

Some people are more naturally disposed to getting in front of camera or standing up in front of people and talking about themselves or their business. If you're not one of those people, you're going to be at a significant disadvantage.

If you are worried about becoming so visible, there really is no need. Any fear you have may be over how you are judged, whether you feel you have anything to say or if you're worried you are going to damage your brand if you don't present yourself in a certain way will disappear when you get results.

You can achieve more in one 60-second video shot on your iPhone and posted on Facebook in front of your audience than spending several thousand pounds on advertising for marketing. A scattergun approach doesn't achieve anything or spending hours networking where you are left practically begging for business from people.

The most important thing is "being seen".

All the social media platforms recognise there is huge value on people posting videos and content. They actively want you to create content for your audience in order to keep people engaged on the platform and will reward you with greater exposure.

You have to use this to your advantage.

This is why so many coaches, consultants and entrepreneurs get it completely wrong. They mistake the need to get in front of the audience with a desire to be famous the world over.

You don't need to be famous to the world. You just need to be famous to your perfect customer, whether that's 10 people 100 people or a thousand people.

If you've done any speaking before, you realise the power of being up on the stage. Simply being stood on the stage confers on you an authority over the audience sitting watching you. You have (literally) been positioned beneficially in front of those individuals by virtue of your where you're stood.

**The first business event I promoted, the Traffic & Lead Gen Bootcamp.**

The same applies to video. Seeing you talking on video on a regular basis, regardless of what you actually say or share, will eventually position you as "famous" to the right audience if you engage them.

We've all experienced the power of social networks. It's odd at first when you meet people you never knew who come up to you to speak with you about something you had written months ago or talk to you about something you wrote about on your Instagram feed.

When you scale back your ambitions for being world-renowned to just focusing on the audience that matters, it takes the pressure off.

Ultimately, what you're trying to do with video is to use content to position you as an expert – which you will do using the strategy I explain in a moment. Really what you're trying to do is establish yourself as an inspirational character or personality worth listening to. Someone they can emotionally invest in.

You may be the most knowledgeable expert on the planet but if you don't bring any authenticity or emotion with you in the way that you put yourself out, there people will simply not follow you. People who are NOT following you, are not listening to you. If they're not listening to you they will most certainly not buy from you.

**Everything starts with:**

- Establishing credibility
- Strengthening trust, and
- Building a human connection

Let's look at how you can do that simply with all the content you put out.

# 1. Share your value

You're an expert.

You possess a body of knowledge and expertise that can make a huge difference to the lives of those you choose to work with and who pay you well.

So, what do you do? Keep your knowledge under lock and key and hold onto it for yourself only releasing your innermost secrets and strategies to paying customers? Or do you give it all away (or at least most of it)?

If you think keeping your cards close to your chest is the way forward, you're in for a shock. Sharing your knowledge and value is the quickest route to earning six figures and above… and I'll tell you why.

These days you have to overcome two problems: increasingly skeptical audiences and other competition in the market

vying for the same customers you're targeting. There is only one strategy that costs absolutely nothing, is practically zero effort from your point of view and gives you a unique selling point your competitors cannot emulate: YOU.

Simply share your knowledge, give advice and provide value BEFORE you bring someone on as a customer. Prove to them by giving them a small portion of a result you want and demonstrate you're worth what you charge.

If you follow my business Facebook page for Rocket Marketing Hub, you will see more than 90% of all videos and content published fits into the category of advice or information. I spend enough time making sure you get real value from each video.

It's not about simply talking about a problem. If you solve their problems BEFORE they become a customer, they stick with you forever.

## 2. Deliver insight

Give a prospect an "aha" moment and they'll listen to you forever.

This supports the point above about sharing value. Going beyond sharing information and advice as another way of rapidly building trust and relationships with your audience is to deliver insights to them about the challenge they face.

This could be something as simple as explaining complex ideas and elements to throw light on a solution. It may mean simplifying complicated ideas and concepts so they understand they can do it themselves. It may also mean curating content to give them an insight quickly.

Your aim is to provide them with a series of "a-ha" moments in the time they spend with you online.

The idea is to help re-frame how they see their world. You do that by delivering insights that break down their existing frames (or misconceptions) and rebuild them in a different way.

Battle to blast away myths by telling them about erroneous advice others have given or failed to show them. Rebuild their understanding of the situation to benefit them and it puts you in a strong position. It rapidly builds trust, builds relationships and transforms you into the "go to" person they think of whenever they have a problem related to the challenge you solve.

## 3. Show them everything, warts and all

Show them the human behind the personality and they'll watch you forever.

I spent a huge amount of time creating videos both recorded and on Facebook live and sharing them with my Facebook community, Advanced Business Growth. Creating these videos and preparing for them took a considerable amount of time. When they were published I was pleased to say they got good engagement, lots of shares and feedback.

If you want to see this type of engagement in action, join the Advanced Business Growth group here:

www.facebook.com/groups/advancedbusinessgrowth

I test with lots of different types of posts all the time.

I can say, without a doubt, the posts which show my personality or personal side are consistently the most commented on, the most shared and the most liked.

Again, it goes to show that human interest drives ongoing engagement. While people may come to you for advice and help, they will keep coming back because they connect with you as a person.

Here's a perfect example.

I spent three days presenting at one of our small business digital marketing events in London and much of the day my face was plastered all over social media, either by my team or through photos taken at the event by attendees. We also put out a lot of video and photo content for those who didn't attend so they received a lot of value even though they weren't there - delivering useful advice while also promoting attendance at our events.

The posts we published had good engagement and I was happy with the way they got our message across about the event. But nothing got quite the engagement as this one photo I posted at home later on that evening...

Yes, it's a picture of me with my dog at home. Perhaps it's because people see me with a dog, they think of their own dog and that makes them smile. Perhaps it's because it shows me off the stage and in a relaxed, switched-off setting that builds a stronger connection to the reader.

Whatever the reason, it's a post that inspires emotion. When you engage your readers' emotional core, you develop a stronger relationship and bond with your audience.

That's why you should never worry about sharing more of you and your life with your followers as possible. It's the small moments of vulnerability and when you're switched-off that really build the connection and strengthen their relationship with you.

A word of warning, though. Make sure it is authentic. One of my biggest bugbears is seeing entrepreneurs faking their authenticity, talking about their struggle while walking along a tropical beach or giving advice about "keeping it real" while sitting in their Bentley. It's patronising and everyone sees right through it.

Just show yourself and share what you're doing on a regular basis and let your tribe buy into you.

# STRATEGY #2
# SELL MORE BY SELLING LESS

How do you sell?

If you've tried growing a business or starting up on your own or even trying to work yourself you'll know that the most important process is sales. What really makes selling difficult if you're not sales professional is knowing when to ask for the sale.

The common mistake non-sales professionals make, and indeed most experts make, is trying to ask for the sale too early.

Trying to sell yourself by putting out direct offers to your audience on social media or other channels is often what most people *think* they need to be doing.

The problem with this approach is it only really appeals to individuals who are ready to buy, and only if they're ready to buy from you immediately. In any situation, only 3% of people are ready to buy what you want right now. This leaves 97% of readers or viewers who may not be ready by right now.

If you constantly sell online by pushing your offer into people's faces, you will quickly discover this approach does not work. Surprisingly, even though they know this approach doesn't deliver results many freelancers, coaches, consultants and entrepreneurs persist with it. Throwing out offers all the time is an easy default. But you're not just failing to make sales; you're actively damaging your business.

Not only does it immediately alienate people, it also has the unintended side-effect of de-positioning you. To see you constantly everywhere trying to SELL, SELL, SELL seriously undermines your position as an expert.

The best way to sell your services or your product is to be more strategic about what you say and when you say it.

Selling more and putting out more offers, more regularly will not result in more sales. Quite counterintuitively, you will sell more by selling LESS.

Here's what I mean by that.

Think of it like a date. If you're going on a date with someone, would you ask them to get married on that very first date?

I like to think most people who say "no" to the question, despite how much of a whirlwind romance it may be. Just like a dating scenario, the same applies to the relationship between you and your audience. Going in for a sale the first time they interact with you is the equivalent of trying to get married on the first date.

Building a relationship with another person takes time. You have to take time to learn about each other, share some information, discover what you're both like.

Yes, your enthusiastic selling approach may feel like it's working in terms of the energy you put into it. You would *think* your chances of success would be high by increasing the number of people you sell to. But online it simply doesn't work like that.

If you took a different approach and got to know people better before popping the big question (i.e. asking for the sale) then your success rate will rise.

Change how you think. Instead of trying to sell something something really start building the relationship.

The first step is not even thinking about the sale at any point in his first few interactions.

Instead force yourself into giving away value first. Show your expertise and experience by giving away advice, insight and allowing the person to know you better.

Giving away a piece of information that interests them or advice that helps them is the best ways to warm an audience to you.

In my business and from my own experience the majority of people who signed up for Rocket Marketing Hub or became clients will have "met" me first online through either watching one of my videos, reading a blog or hearing me speak at an event..

None of them will have interacted with me and found that I tried to sell to them on that first opportunity. It's much better to take a strategic approach, so you are firmly positioned as the expert to help your audience before there is any talk or discussion about buying.

Gary Vaynerchuk, an expert on selling on social media, has a strategy called "Jab, Jab, Jab, Hook" which talks about how you need to earn the right to make an offer to the audience. In this case, you need to give value disproportionately more than you go for the sale.

Give them valuable high-quality content in advance of them ever working with you. It builds rapport and they discover exactly what you can do to help them before ever going to them with an offer of some kind.

The beauty of this "selling more by selling less" approach is that it takes away one of the areas of business that so many of us have trouble with: selling on the phone or in person. If you take this approach you will position yourself so well with your target audience that when it eventually comes to the sale you find closing is much easier and you're not chasing the sale or begging for business.

Very quickly, this strategy shows you that you need not spend hours and hours calling, chasing and following up prospects. All this effort is ultimately wasted if customers don't eventually buy from you. With this "sell less" approach you will increase sales in your business while reducing the amount of time and effort spent selling, freeing you up to work on your areas of strength.

# STRATEGY #3
# PICK THE RIGHT CUSTOMER

One of the biggest mistakes of people who want to become experts in their field is believing they can help everybody.

Now the truth is you probably do give a shit about the value of what you do. You probably are an expert in your field. You probably could help nearly everybody in some way. And you could probably turn most people into a customer if you pitched your services in the right way. However, the important thing to remember is the use of the word "could". Just because you *could* doesn't mean you should.

Many people who want to become an expert and make huge amounts of money from their coaching consulting business fall into the trap of casting their net too wide.

It's understandable. I can completely relate. On the face of it, it makes sense that to win more business, you need to appeal to as many people as possible who can pay. In fact, the opposite is true. To win more business you need to very closely target the kind of person that you would like to work with.

There is good reason for this, as I will explain.

When you try to work with everyone you end up working with no one.

I know this from bitter experience. I learnt this lesson very quickly when I decided to start my digital marketing agency.

When I opened my doors on the first day, I knew I could work with nearly every single business with an online presence. I was confident I could deliver a huge amount of value to anyone who wanted to work with me. I knew I could very quickly get real results for any business I met at a networking event or came across in my everyday life.

The problem was this: because my target was too broad, so was my message.

I struggled to connect to businesses in certain sectors - such as accounting or retail - because my communication didn't sound as though I fully understood the concerns of those sectors. I struggled to compete against other agencies that were sector specialists. They were able to speak to potential clients in a language they both understood. As a result, they would always win pitches over me.

When it comes to marketing, this is a very important lesson to be learnt: to rapidly increase the rate of your growth specialise - or niche - as quickly as possible.

To use a medical analogy, surgeons who specialise in operations are paid significantly more than general practitioners. The same applies with nearly every profession: the specialists are ALWAYS paid more than the generalists.

When marketing yourself and promoting your business, this is even more important. Only when I understood this lesson did my business start to gain traction. For months, I toiled away trying to win business for my digital marketing agency with no luck.

Once I decided to pick a niche and target one part of the market very specifically did I start winning client after client after client.

It's obvious when you see the situation from the other side. Whenever my agency was pitching against another (generalist) agency it was much easier for me to speak in specifics to my potential customer. It was far more powerful for me to articulate how I could help them because I was part of their industry. I used their language. I understood the market conditions. I could speak to them with a deeper understanding and knowledge about their challenges than I would had I remained a generalist.

You *can* succeed without niching - and many businesses have successfully grown who operate in the whole market - but they are exceptions. If you have limited resources, want to grow quickly and win more customers, choosing a more closely-defined audience will get you there faster.

If you don't niche, it also becomes difficult to scale up when you need to and grow your business exponentially.

Now, if this is all a bit scary, let me set your mind at ease. Just because you are narrowing your target audience doesn't mean you can't work with people outside of that target audience. For our purposes, you are being super-targeted about who you work with because it is easier in the long-term to target a well-defined audience segment with the tools of digital marketing.

People, who want to work with you, will want to work with you regardless of your niche.

There is nothing stopping you with working with lots of smaller niches. Once you realise the power of being really targeted - in terms of your content output, your marketing and your message - you'll see the benefits they will bring.

If you're worried about choosing the wrong niche or one that isn't big enough to support your ambitious company growth, here's my advice:

Start by working on one target audience and do everything you can to make that a success, and only then move onto appealing to another. This way you won't feel like you're narrowing the scope of your work but you'll see the effect of being super-targeted in your approach. And very quickly.

You may be asking "what was your niche, James"?

Well, when I learnt this secret almost overnight I got very specific about who we talked it. My agency eventually focused on working with double glazing companies who wanted greater local presence, SEO and digital marketing. (How's that for super specific?)

The real benefit from picking a niche and working on it, is you can really leverage testimonials and case studies because they appeal to others in that niche and sell you like gangbusters. Most businesses don't think marketers understand their sector. By showing them case studies of businesses just like theirs we'd helped, they couldn't do anything else but pick up the phone to us and asked what we could do for them. That's powerful positioning in action.

Remember, this is only the start of the journey. It will help you reach your income goals much quicker and give you the freedom you've always craved.

In every case, it's better to be a big fish in a small pond than a small fish in an ocean. Choosing your audience wisely is the first step.

As I finish this section, let me give an example to see how this may work in practice.

Put yourself in the shoes of a female executive - let's call her Jane - who has lost a job in the city and now wants to start her own business.

She doesn't know anything about setting up or running a business after so many years in the corporate world. Therefore, she already knows she needs a coach to help with her business set-up and launch, so she goes searching online and finds three possible coaches who could help her.

The first coach visits her. She tells her about her experience working with all kinds of businesses run by all kinds of people in every sector, selling her versatility and broad experience as one of her major reasons why she's the best option.

The second business coach she speaks with is a coach who specialises in only working with women in business. The coach talks in detail through the specific challenges women face as entrepreneurs and how her experience working exclusively with women gives her an understanding of the common challenges and self-limiting beliefs female entrepreneurs have. To Jane, this coach seems more in tune with her specific needs than the first coach.

However, the third coach tells Jane something different again. She is a coach specialising in working with women who previously worked for major corporations and were looking to set up their own business as an entrepreneur. When she meets Jane she presents specific case studies of three different women who worked for similar size companies that Jane worked at and talked in detail about the key frustrations they commonly felt. Jane listens to the third coach and it sounds like someone is talking about her - her professional and personal situation as well as reading back her exact feelings and frustrations.

Of the three, the coach with the more narrow niche was able to speak more effectively to Jane and ultimately sell her on working with her.

Now you can see the difference picking a more targeted audience can make. The only caveat to this is always making sure there is financial opportunity in the niche you pick and the market is big enough.

If you're selling pet accessories to every pet owner in the UK you're going to go broke (or mad) trying to appeal to the whole market - unless you have a huge marketing team behind you and bottomless funds.

If you're trying to sell doggie pyjamas to vegan owners of overweight Dachshunds in London, you'll struggle to find a market big enough to support a growing business (although you're sure to make one dog owner very, very happy).

The next question invariably becomes: how do I identify the right customer and find out more about them? That's where the Customer Avatar becomes important.

Here's the part every business tries to skip and very few take the time to do. The crazy thing is that without doing a customer profile (or avatar), your business won't know who it needs to attract as it hasn't been put on paper.

Getting it down somewhere is an important step as it will clarify the three most important pillars of who you want to work with, what you need to say and how you can reach them. Get these fixed before you do anything else.

## How to create the perfect customer avatar

A customer avatar is a detailed profile of the sort of person you want to be your ideal customer.

When you have a customer avatar in place, you will be able to:

- Reach out to and service a niche where you are recognised as the leading expert
- Craft your marketing message so it appeals to a specific person as opposed to being a generic message
- Boost your conversion rates by saying the right things that generate action
- Reach out to more of the right sort of customers because the "wrong" buyer will not be interested in what you have to say
- Save money because you will not be spending money on marketing activities that don't work

You will find that it is simple to create a customer avatar. All you need to do is fill out a template based on information that will help you to profile your most valued customer. At the end of this chapter, I'll share with you a link where you can download a free template to help you create your own customer avatar.

If you think that you don't need an avatar because your business appeals to everyone, you are making a MASSIVE MISTAKE.

This is only true for the handful of businesses that are genuinely in the mass market business. If you were to closely examine your customer base, you will find that you have a core group that:

- Spends more than the rest of your customers
- Provides you with repeat sales
- Will upgrade to the premium services or products you offer
- Will generate a sizeable proportion of your profits, and they won't barter on the price
- Will provide you with tremendous feedback
- Are really good to work with

Additionally, you will find these customers spread the word about your business to their friends and family members. This means that you will be found on social media, drawing more people to you. When you look closely at your customers, you will find these buyers will very likely share demographics in common, they will often hold similar values and they will be motivated by similar things.

If you then compare these aspects to the people that only buy one product from you, who are much more demanding and who leave you feeling unsettled or uncomfortable, you should find that the profile of these people isn't the same as the profile of the core group for your business.

By focusing all of your attention on your core customer group, you will be able to attract the right people and give them exactly what they are looking for.

You'll find that if you construct your own detailed customer avatar, you will stand apart from your peers and rivals. This is because few businesses take this step or make the effort. This means that by taking this step, you can provide yourself with a competitive advantage. A detailed customer avatar will guarantee you are:

- Using the language that your customers use and feel comfortable with
- Addressing the buying objections of your customers and assuring them that you can solve their issues
- Creating the sort of offer that your ideal customer will respond to
- Filtering out the sort of customers that you would prefer to not work with

So what goes into a customer avatar? Three elements, predominantly, and the more detailed you are, the better the results from your efforts. Here's what you need to sketch out:

- **Demographics** - the demographic details are about who they are and will be used to define their situation. These may seem very basic but are essential to understand exactly who you appeal to. Questions include: Who is your customer? What age are they? Where do they live? Are they single or married? How big is their family? What do they earn? What is their profession? Where do they live? What size home do they live in?

- **Psychographics** - these are how your customer feels, which is really important when knowing how to craft your message. People buy on emotions and justify on logic. Humans are not rational beings. You need to appeal to your customer on an emotional level and only through understanding their emotional state can you really understand how to speak with them. Questions include: What are their current frustrations and challenges? What keeps them up at night? What do they about when they wake up in the morning? What are their desires, wants and needs? What do they like and dislike (not just about your product but in general)?

- **Behaviour** - understanding your customer's behaviour is vital to knowing where to reach them and how. If we know they read a certain newspaper, you know that is how to get in front of them. You also know what appeals to them. Questions include: Where do they get their news? What do they read? What car do they drive? What do they talk about at home? Where do they shop? What social networks do they use?

- **Objections** - knowing what prevents your customer from buying is just as important as what triggers a purchase. Questions include: How do they make buying decisions? Who do they listen to? What stop them from purchasing? What are their common objections?

And, finally, here's the important bit. Once you have completed the profile, be sure to name your avatar. This will further place the image of your customer in your mind. You should then look to post a picture of your avatar in a prominent place in your workspace, as this will provide you with a constant reminder of who you are working towards. You should have this customer in mind every time you:

- Create a blog post
- Write new copy
- Develop new products or services

You need to make the effort to think about your customer and understand things from their perspective. If you do this you will find that you will have a much greater chance of reaching out to a customer with success. When you meet the needs of your customer, you will have a positive impact on your bottom line and it will make the rest of your marketing system much more effective.

**FREE CUSTOMER AVATAR TEMPLATE DOWNLOAD** >> This is a serious opportunity to significantly improve your business, and by downloading the free template, you can have a positive impact on your business. Your template is available by going here:

r o c k e t m a r k e t i n g h u b . c o m / craft_the_perfect_customer_avatar/

Now you've picked your audience the next strategy is all about knowing the right way to talk to them...

# STRATEGY #4
# SELL THE RESULT, NOT THE PRODUCT OR SERVICE

When I was running my iPhone accessories retail company, my entire marketing communication was focused on making my customers aware of the specific products and product features of each of the items we were selling. If you wanted a silicon case, that is how we sold it - here's a silicone case. If you wanted an extra-long iPhone charger cable that's how it was sold - here's a charger cable.

It sounds obvious. You sell something; surely it's a case of telling people exactly what they're getting and all the features?

That's what I thought. Here's the problem. When you think in terms of features, you become a commodity. And commodities end up being compared on price. I don't want that for you. It wasn't until a spoke to a copywriter that I fully understood that people do not buy products and services…

**People buy outcomes and results.**

All successful business is about transformation. You are in the business of moving your customer from A to B, where "A" is their present situation and "B" is the desired outcome.

If you can move a person from a "Before" state to the "After" state that they want, you get choose your price. For the "Before" state, the customer will be unhappy or have a desire that is going unfulfilled. It may be they are bored, tired, frightened or in pain. For the "After" state, the life of the buyer is improved and you help them move from the state that troubled them to a happier position.

People will buy into how well you promise them the "After" state. If you have a brilliant offer, people will naturally move towards the "After" state and if you have strong marketing, you will be in a position to articulate this move from "Before" to "After". This is where many businesses fail and they fail because:

- They don't have an offer that will move someone to the "After" state.

- The marketing fails to describe the movement from "Before" to "After"

- You have to be clear about the outcome your offer provides to people

While this book shows you how to position yourself as an expert and then use digital marketing systems to attract and win customers, the message and words you use to describe how you benefit your ultimate customer is the most important factor in whether you will make a lot of money or get left behind.

The right message that spells out the benefits of working with you is more important than all the technology and systems I show you in this book. A great marketing message without a system may still allow you to sell what you do… but a great marketing system with the wrong target market or a message that doesn't speak to your customers' desires will NEVER sell.

That's why it's worth spending time getting this right at the beginning. To do that, you need to be clear in what you ultimately offer. To get this clarity, ask yourself these questions:

- What does the customer have in the "Before" state and what does the customer have in the "After" state?

- How does your customer feel in the "Before" state and how do they feel in the "After" state?

- What makes up an average day for your customer in the "Before" state and what makes up an average day for your customer in the "After" state?

- What is the status of your customer in the "Before" state and what is the status of your customer in the "After" state?

A good way to lay-out these questions is to use a before and after grid so you can lay out the answers side by side, making it easier to tell the difference between the two responses.

| | Before | After |
|---|---|---|
| Have | | |
| Feel | | |
| Av Day | | |
| Status | | |

As an example, think about a business that sells marketing services. Being profitable is hugely important for any business owner, but it can be difficult and challenging. You are looking to move your clients from loss-making to profitable. Your clients struggling get by and you need to get them to the "After" state, where they now have customers on demand.

Look at their "Before" and "After" state in relation to four things: what they HAVE, what they FEEL, their AVERAGE DAY and their STATUS.

To answer the above questions:

- You are moving the business owner from HAVING no customers or very few to HAVING high-quality customers on demand
- You are moving the business owner from FEELING stressed and worried to FEELING confident and in control

- You are moving the business owner from having an AVERAGE DAY that was challenging to having an AVERAGE DAY where they are spending quality time growing their business.
- You are moving the business owners from a STATUS of feeling embarrassed to a STATUS of feeling on top of the world.

The minimum level of marketing that many businesses undertake will only state what a customer will have if they buy the product or service. Experts that make serious money and never struggle for clients will be able to tell a customer how they feel, how their average day can be improved and how their status will be positively impacted upon by working with them.

The change from "before" to "after" is crucial and this should now come across in your copy. A good copywriter will be able to create a marketing message that impacts on the customer. Having done the exercise above, here's how that message now sounds…

*"Making your business profitable with customers on demand, doesn't have to be a difficult and scary challenge. Banish the stress of running your business! By knowing exactly how many customers you will attract each month you can remove the guesswork from running your business. Your business will benefit from being able to control the flow of customers to the business. Gone are the days of feast and famine"*

These examples move the business owner from "Before" to "After", removing the stress and strain of the situation and making things better for the business.

You will also find that the movement from "Before" to After" can also impact on how much you can charge for your product. (Hint: if you're like most experts I work with you probably seriously undervalue what you're worth and you probably need to be charging more for your products and services). The distance between the "Before" and "After" states is recognised as VALUE.

This is great news for you. Because if you want to charge a higher price for the product or services you offer, create more distance between the "Before" and "After" state. You can do this by:

- Making a better offering (product or service)
- Clearly articulate the movement from "Before" to "After"
- Keep things simple

You also want to make sure that you are clear with respect to the "Before" and "After". If you are unable to do this, you may not have the right product to market fit. If you are unable to get this stage right, you may struggle at every point because the system and process is dependent on having access to a group of people that are willing and able to buy.

# STRATEGY #5
# INCREASE CUSTOMER VALUE
# THROUGH THE VALUE LADDER

There's one thing better than a fully engaged fan of your work… and that's a customer. And there is one thing even better than a customer… and that's a repeat customer.

Understanding how to move a reader who is interested in what you have to say through to becoming a customer who buys from you again and again goes to the heart of what this book is about.

You're an expert and you deserve to be well paid for your expertise and experience and how much you can help those you choose to work with. But here's what happens in the case of many freelancers, entrepreneurs, coaches, consultants or other expert businesses.

You start out with great enthusiasm hoping to serve as many people as possible. You know you can make a difference to the lives of those you work with. Business kicks off well and you have a couple of clients. As you help those clients make breakthroughs and go off and make a better life for themselves, you have a problem. There's no pipeline of new leads or customers flowing into the business. It's feast and famine.

You think that perhaps with your case studies and success stories, business would naturally gravitate towards you. It doesn't. Week after week goes by with leads trickling in painfully. You try to understand why people aren't buying from you. You ask a couple of leads who didn't buy and they tell you "price".

So you lower your prices, you make-do. A new client now signs up at a lower rate. Immediately, you regret it. They feel you owe them much more than they paid. They take up more and more of your time… but what can you do? You need to pay your rent or mortgage.

All the other leads you desperately want to say YES to you, aren't getting back to you. It may be your price or something else but they are taking a long time to convert. All the while you're working with lowball clients who hold your business back.

This doesn't need to be a reality. All you need is a simple, predictable system that positions you perfectly in front of your audience and delivers you a stream of valuable leads who are able to make increasingly larger purchases with you until they are prepared to pay you several thousand pounds for your time.

As an expert, you shouldn't be wasting your time personally selling low value products. Instead, you should be creating digital or physical products which you can sell to potential prospects earlier on in the relationship with you. These will effectively qualify prospects and you don't have to administer them or personally sell them.

That is where the ascending value ladder comes in. And here's an example of one at work:

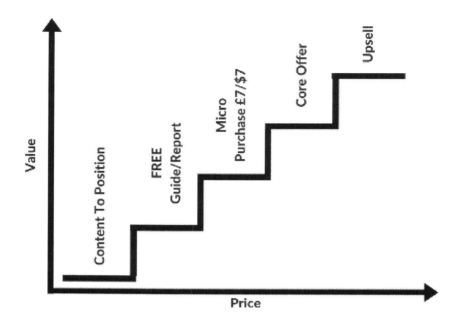

It works on a basis of common sense.

You have a Core Offer, which is the main offer in your business. If you are a coach or consultant this may be an hour of your time, a coaching programme or a day of consulting. Whatever it is, this will be your signature product or service for which you most likely charge several thousand pounds.

If you were to ask someone who needed a coach or consultant but didn't know you to take your Core Offer right away, they may be reluctant. They will have all manner of objections and worries they want answered before handing over any amount of money.

Questions like: Are you any good? What do I get working with you? Have you helped others like me? And so on - all the objections and obstacles to purchase you highlighted when you wrote your Customer Avatar.

Wouldn't it be better to transform their experience? What if you could first get them to invest only a small amount of money with you to help them deal with the problem they're facing… possibly only a few pounds. For them, the risk is much, much lower, yet the benefit is high.

This is the purpose of the ascending value ladder. To sell a potential customer something high in value but small in price. This makes it as easy for the customer to invest in you as possible and take the first step.

Once someone hands over their cash or credit card details, making the second or third and every sale thereafter becomes increasingly easy.

It's all down to human psychology. When someone buys from you, something magical happens. They're 10 times more likely to buy from you again compared with someone who has NEVER bought from you.

Later in this book, I show you the complete marketing system I use in my business and teach to other expert businesses, but it hinges on this strategy. Making someone a customer so you can sell to them again more easily is what will propel your business forward.

That's why the first step in a value ladder is a low-ball but high value purchase. They need to buy something early on that is disproportionately valuable. So much so, it's a NO BRAINER for them. We're talking about something around the £7 or less mark.

What could something at the low end of the value ladder be? Well it could be a training video or a book or a short training course. Basically, it needs to demonstrate you know what you're talking about and that you can be trusted, while also helping them solve a part of the problem. For example, if you are a sales trainer you may sell a "closing on the phone" script video workshop for £7, which will help your potential customer successfully learn part of the bigger solution. It doesn't give them the WHOLE solution, but it deepens the trust they have that you're the right person to help them as you already have.

As you'll see when we talk in more detail about a system, starting off with a low offer encourages an interested individual to buy from you sooner. It's a lower financial risk and as soon as that initial transaction is made, they are psychologically invested.

When you then go back to them - and this may be almost immediately AFTER they make the first purchase - you can start to ask them to invest a little bit more each time until they are ready to receive the main offer.

For example, the value ladder for my business will look like something similar to this:

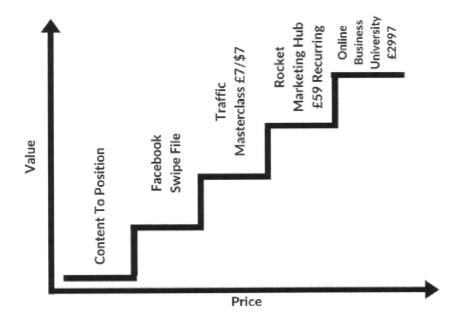

The reader will make a small commitment by downloading a book on Facebook with a number of examples of Facebook advertising.

We call this a lead magnet, as the commitment is their contact details.

The lead magnet is a great enticement that provides a large level of value to a potential customer in exchange for information that they hold, usually their email address and name.

While no money changes hands at this point, it IS a transaction and it is normally the very first transaction you have with a customer.

It is important to provide great value with a lead magnet. The lead magnet is normally provided on a web page that is referred to as a squeeze page or a landing page, and this page will have been optimised to convert leads. You don't need a fancy landing page, it just needs to do the task that you need it to.

Almost immediately after they download the lead magnet they will be asked if they want to take advantage of a super-low priced Facebook training programme which only costs £7.

This training will be worth WAY MORE than £7 but the price point is designed to make this a crazy offer they can't refuse. At a £7 price point, a certain proportion of those downloaders of the swipe book will pay £7 and become customers. They have taken the important step and it has been enough for them to trust I can deliver that value in the £7 course.

Now, they will have the course, but they will be made an offer to join Rocket Marketing Hub for £59/month subscription. Again this may be done immediately or soon after purchase of the £7 product.

Here's the important part: it doesn't matter whether they've actually used the £7 training. All that matters is the fact they were prepared to pay you money that breaks that psychological barrier and allows them to trust you to purchase again. When we go back with the £59/month offer we know the majority of people have NOT used the £7 product, but their purchase highlights they believe they need it because there is a challenge in their business.

With the Rocket Marketing Hub offer we put to them, it acknowledges they have an issue that needs resolution and gives them a way to speed up the resolution of that part of the problem. That's exactly how your value ladder needs to work. As your customer ascends the ladder, the solution becomes easier and more certain the more they invest.

The ascending value ladder may even include elements within it that don't necessarily involve financial cost but time cost. For example, here's another value ladder within my business:

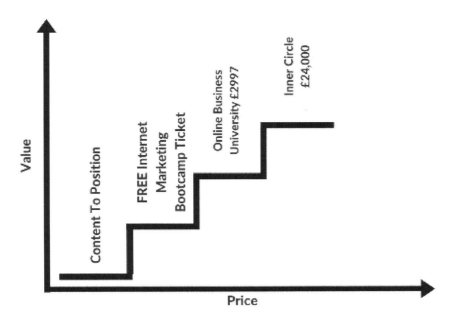

For someone to spend a whole day of their time at one of our Internet Marketing Bootcamp events in London is a big commitment for most people. That's why when they do, they're proving themselves to be more committed and invested than others who prefer to just watch online or consume your free content hoping for help.

When you put an offer to a more invested group of people, you will get better results when selling them higher ticket items.

An example value ladder for your business may be something along these lines:

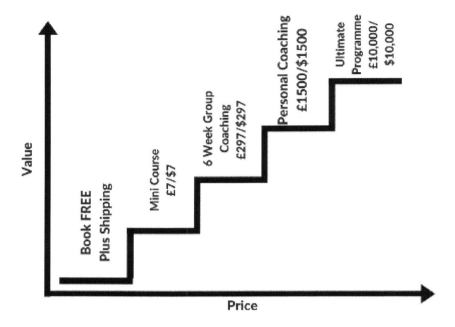

Notice how in this example, you're not actually working one-on-one with anyone until the price point of £1500 has been reached. That means the earlier stages of your value ladder and your interaction with your target audience can either be automated or leveraged in terms of your time so you're getting in front of multiple people without taking up your time or reducing the value of working one-to-one with you.

Think now as to your own personal value ladder. What assets, products or programmes do you have in your business right now you can use to create a value ascension ladder that brings a potential new customer into your world and let's them buy from you without you being involved?

Take a piece of paper and try sketching out some possible value ladders in your business and how that would look. This will help later in the book when we start designed the system to put this into action.

Having something to sell in the first place is great. But you need someone to sell it to and put it in front of. That's why the next strategy is so important…

# STRATEGY #6
# BUILD YOUR AUDIENCE ALL THE TIME

You can't make a noise if you don't have an audience to speak to.

Most people are invisible. Most businesses are invisible. Most experts are invisible.

As part of my work I undertake a huge number of marketing consults with businesses all over the UK and the world. Most of these companies are really good. They have great products and services. They have great people working in the business. They have a really good message and they know what to say to prospects to persuade them to buy.

On the face of it, these businesses appear to be doing everything right, yet they're surprised they have difficulty attracting leads and winning customers. What really shocks them is seeing lesser competition winning business ahead of them. They're floored when other businesses they know provide an inferior service or have a history of low customer service keep beating them time and again in the battle for customers. The reason? They're invisible and their competitors are not.

It's never anything to do with how good your product or business is. Everything is about being seen by your customers.

The most successful entrepreneurs leading a business know they need to be visible to customers, prospects and the market as a whole. They make it their job to ensure that visibility is there all the time.

Take Coca-Cola. The drinks giant spends millions and millions of dollars on brand awareness every year. They know they need to maintain visibility all the time in order for people to keep buying their products, otherwise they would simply forget they're there and not buy. That's a brand as big as Coca-Cola!

You may love Coke, but if you're not constantly reminded that it's there you're not always thinking about it in your everyday life. (I'm certainly not going to suggest you spend major amounts of money on brand awareness, but your marketing does need to keep you front of mind so it's worth thinking how brand awareness campaigns work).

This is such a clear lesson yet so few businesses take notice. Most businesses are happy to remain invisible, out of sight and, ultimately, out of mind of the target customer. Really, there is no excuse for this at all.

With today's technology, it's so easy to get in front of a global audience. It's free to communicate your message to need to reach.

Although, at the time of writing, social media platforms like Facebook and LinkedIn are making it increasingly difficult to continue getting free exposure - making you pay for increased visibility and 'reach' - there is certainly still the opportunity to use these technologies to get right in front of your customer.

One of the pillars of the success strategy outlined above is consistency. Persistently and consistently putting yourself and your message in front of our ideal audience is the basis for any long-term success when it comes to marketing yourself. There is no way around this, believe me.

All kinds of marketing experts and Internet gurus will try to tell you there is a way to shortcut this. As if somehow you can put out a couple of blogs and a few videos and it will be enough for streams of traffic to flow to your website or there are secrets to improving your visibility that doesn't involve consistently posting high-quality content about yourself and your business. They are lying to you.

I'm sorry, that's probably not what you want to hear. I'm sorry if you were hoping I was going to share some "secret code" that all online marketers know that tells you how to get visibility without putting the effort in. Unfortunately, there isn't such a code.

(The closest you can get to a shortcut to get in front of your audience is by paying for traffic, but in terms of "free" there is no shortcut).

Before we discuss where to go to communicate with our perfect customer, we need to talk about the different ways of communication. How you talk to your audience and for what purpose is just as important as where you post.

**How to communicate**

There are two main types of communication you need to distinguish between:

- Engagement

- Promotions and offers

Engagement content is designed to get your ideal customer consuming your content, whether that is through blogs, videos and emails. This type of content should be designed to position you as an authority and an expert by sharing your knowledge and insight without the expectation of anything in return. High quality, useful content given to your target audience positions you by letting them know you better, demonstrating your knowledge and letting them spend time with you so you can increase trust and develop a relationship with them.

The purpose of engagement content is to ENGAGE your reader and get them consuming your content to control how they feel about you. The more they feel you're the expert they're looking for, the more likely they are to buy from you in the future.

The purpose of these emails is NOT to generate sales. That is the purpose of promotions and offers.

Promotions and offers are the sales emails and copy in your communication process. You do not want to be putting these to your audience all the time. Your audience need to keep interested and engaged with valuable advice-based content for the majority of their time with you.

Only when you have provided them with good content and offered plenty of free advice, help and value, do you deserve the opportunity to put offers in front of them.

There is a delicate balance between giving away too much value and never going in for the sale. The fact is you need engagement content in your business to be able to make the sale… but if you never attempt to make the sale with offers and promotions you won't have a business. It's important to get this right.

I see so many coaches, consultants and freelancers giving away all their knowledge for free and NEVER trying to sell anything for fear they may alienate or upset their audience. The mad thing is the opposite is often true. If you give away lots of great content and help your audience, you do them a disservice by not offering them a paid way to quickly solve their challenges and they resent you for it.

Regularly schedule in promotions and offers to counterbalance the engagement content to keep bringing in customers to your system and ascending them through the value ladder.

So what do we use to grow our audience and keep their attention?

## How to grow your audience

Right now, there are four ways which are working best to get in front of your audience, build a relationship with them by sharing content and also bringing them into your value ladder. These are:

- Blogs
- Email
- Video
- Facebook Groups

Let's break these down and go into detail about why you benefit from focusing on these different ways of building your audience.

## Blogs

Blogging is one of the most effective ways of both positioning yourself as an expert in your field and engaging your audience and sharing your knowledge. Using your own website, you can create regular posts that answer the specific problems and challenges of your audience.

When it comes to creating blog content, there are so many great reasons to start now, including:

- Providing content to an email list
- Making offers and placing them in the content
- Retargeting visitors

Blogging is one of those activities that sounds like a lot of work. When you are so busy, it can be really hard to find the time to create the great content you need. It doesn't have to be hard, you just need a little inspiration to get started. Flip to Appendix I with a comprehensive list of ideas to get started blogging.

These are just some of the immediate reasons you need to create blog posts. Here are five ways to create blog posts without having to write thousands of words:

*1. Embedded blog posts.*

This is really simple. Go to Youtube and find a really high quality video that features someone who is regarded as an authority in your niche or sector. Embed this video into your blog and then beneath the video, write a reaction or analysis of the video.

## 2. Aggregate content

If you feel as though you don't have the time to create content, this is a great step because you don't have to create content. All you do is aggregate it from other sources around the web.

Find great content that can be linked to a theme and always make sure that you credit the original source with a link. This is essential. You have to link it back to the source, but when you pull in content from so many places, people will appreciate having so much information in one place.

## 3. Interview blog posts

This is a great way to create content that is relevant and that people want to read. You may also find that people at a very high level in your industry will be happy to be interviewed. It is so much easier to convince someone to be interviewed than it is to ask them to write something for you. If you are keen to have an authoritative name on your site, this is likely to be the most sensible option.

There are plenty of ways in which you can conduct an interview but you will find that recorded audio over the phone is the simplest. This means that the expert doesn't have to write anything, they don't need a webcam, they don't even need to wear clothes if they don't want to.

When you have the full interview, transcribe it and place the interview on site. You can even place the audio on the site as well.

## 4. Quotes

This is a simple way to create content but it gives you a chance to leverage a number of experts in your field. Decide on the topic for your post and then find quotes that are relevant to your post. Then you should place all of these quotes on the same page.

You can add graphics or post your own thoughts and comments if you desire but there is a lot to be said for letting the quotes do the talking.

## 5. Crowdsourced blog posts

A fast and effective way to create a blog post is to ask a number of experts or relevant people the same question. You should then pull these answers together to create a single article showcasing a number of viewpoints in your industry or area.

A good way to do this is to set up an email template and then send it out to noted experts or relevant people. The following is an example of what you want to send:

*"Dear [name]*

*I'm a big fan of your work and I'd like to introduce my audience to your work and your opinions. This will not take a long time. I am creating an article about [chosen subject] and I'd love to have your opinion on a few questions.*

*Could you please provide an answer to the following question in 3 to 5 sentences?*

*[insert question]*

*I would be extremely honoured if you could take part.*

*[your name]"*

You should look to send the email personally and make sure that you flatter the recipient. Be sure to ask them a question that they will have an opinion on.

If you have already received responses, be sure to mention the relevant names. You can do this as many times as you like until you get a good number of responses from which to create a good post.

*6. How To/Advice blog posts*

The really obvious type of blog which will probably take up the most of your time will be help or advice blogs where you get to showcase your expertise.

A really good rule for these is instead of trying to cover as much as possible in any one blog, try to aim for each blog post to cover a single point or argument.

It's all too easy to get bogged down in details and process. What your audience really wants to know about is how to solve their problems. Talk about their problems in terms they understand, then tell them how they can be helped.

**Email**

It has been heavily vilified for both being prone to spam but also blamed for the overwhelm in our daily lives - the dreaded email inbox.

Forget everything you've heard or have been told about whether email marketing works or not. It's not true. Email marketing still represents the most powerful, cost effective way of building a relationship with your target audience and moving them to buy from you.

Having that more intimate relationship in their inbox also has an incredible R.O.I. as you're not paying to put your message to them, unlike Facebook ads or Youtube advertising. It's almost free advertising and all it costs is their email address.

As we'll see, there is a cost to acquiring that email but working with a marketing system you can quickly and cheaply find the right audience, capture their email and start working to build trust, overcome objections and get them to buy.

The most important element here is CAPTURE. Capturing their email address is vital to everything else in this marketing system. Only once you have their email address can you really start to make the relationship work.

Yes, this is changing a great deal. Depending on how well you understand digital marketing there are other ways to automatically track and put messages in front of your customers without requiring their email address and that is through a "pixel".

A retargeting pixel is a piece of code you place on your website or blog that tracks when a visitor views the site or takes an action. It tracks the visitor and then allows you to run advertising to get in front of that reader again.

The smart way to use this is to attract interested individuals to you by creating powerful, helpful content with a pixel, "firing" the pixel when they visit your content and then serving them with advertising which encourages them to download, buy or take another action that allows them to interact with your content again.

But that's just an aside for now, let's get back to the power of email...

Email is powerful for two purposes, both for delivering content and driving readers in your database back to content.

A good email strategy needs to cover lots of bases, the most significant of which is consistent weekly emails designed to engage with those on your list.

Weekly? Well, actually I would suggest daily emails but if you haven't emailed your customers and readers for a while it may be overload. Once a week is a good frequency to aim for and is really the bare minimum.

"But my readers are too busy to read my emails", you may be thinking. Flip that around. Your readers may be too busy to open your email *this* week... but that doesn't matter because they'll get another one from you in seven days which they may even miss again... but then in another seven days when you send another they *do* have time and read your email.

Consistency is key with email marketing because it's not up to you to decide when your customer interacts with your content. It's up to them.

Your job is to be there when they make that decision.

Email marketing is also a powerful tool to drive readers back to your other content, such as blogs, video and lead magnets, so you can get them interacting and active. The more engaged they are, the more likely they will become customers and buy from you.

Regular emails increase the chance of a more highly engaged audience. If you have your content focused on the right audience, this should also put off readers who AREN'T ideal, who will hopefully unsubscribe from your list if the fit isn't right.

Yes, unsubscribes are GOOD news. The last thing you want is to be wasting your time with people who aren't a good fit. How often and how regularly you create and distribute content will make a difference to getting your audience right.

**Our weekly Rocket TV emails**

What should you write in your emails?

That's up to you and the relationship you want with your audience. Your emails can be used simply to share existing content again with your audience or point to new content you have created.

You can write completely original content in your emails to differentiate it from all your other content, making it more personal to reflect the fact you're arriving in their inbox and you already have a relationship with them.

When I use email I employ a combination of both. I regularly share content we've put out on the Rocket Marketing Hub blog and I also write more personal emails that are designed to deepen the relationship I have with my readers - maybe using personal experience.

## Video

Email is great, but there's one medium that will accelerate your positioning and visibility far beyond any other content: video.

Long gone are the days of needing huge investment and camera crews to get your face on a screen in front of an audience. Now, you need your smart phone and an internet connection and you can become a broadcast star to your audience for nothing.

While everyone knows there's no barrier to broadcasting and everyone can get their face on as many platforms as they want, the truth is there is still power in being seen on the screen.

Like watching someone speak from stage, seeing someone's face broadcast on a screen gives them an air of authority you may not experience from simply looking at a written blog.

The power is in the visual and there is a deep-rooted psychological draw to individuals who we see talking with authority.

Video brings advantages and disadvantages. The disadvantage is that getting on video and getting good at video, for most people, will require a leap of faith and stepping out of their comfort zone - at least in the beginning.

But here's the advantage of making video work for you. Most entrepreneurs and experts won't ever dream of getting on camera or making the first step. Or, even if they do it, they'll won't carry it on for more than a few videos. Which means you have the perfect opportunity to own your space.

There are different types of videos you can create and use:

- Straight to video
- Speaking/presentations
- Interviews
- How To
- Customer stories/testimonials

Video gives you a chance to control and edit the content you share. You can use video in different ways to make your audience *feel* a certain way about you.

Here are five different ways we use video to present a powerful message or story, all related to positioning myself as an expert and being visible to my target audience.

*Straight-to-camera advice*

In this series of videos at the Business Show, I share short snippets of advice talking direct to camera. By talking direct to camera it makes it more personal to the audience who feels I'm talking directly to them while positioning me as an expert.

The great thing about these videos was how they gave me authority while also showing how confident I was talking about my subject. Using video to overcome doubts your viewer may have about your ability is powerful.

If you are less than confident on-screen, don't worry. My very first videos were terrible and it took a lot time before I could speak as well as this on camera. It all comes with practice. You just need to start.

You may also be thinking, "when am I going to have the time to record videos like these each week?". That's a good question. The answer is to batch process your video production.

With these videos, I spent a few hours with a videographer at the Business Show and ended up recording about 30 separate videos. Once the videographer edited these we uploaded them to Youtube and scheduled them to automatically publish every week. That means I had over half a year's worth of video content ready to go with less than two hours' time spent recording. Remember, when it comes to content creation, working smarter is the way to go.

*Speaking/presenting/panel discussions*

If you recall what I said about standing on stage, you automatically gain authority with your audience simply through your position up on the stage or behind a lectern. When you capture that on video, it doubles in power.

**Speaking at Traffic & Lead Gen Bootcamp To 200 People**

**Panel discussion at the car show to 400 people**

Sharing video of you speaking to audiences, teaching and sharing will build your authority and positioning and allow the viewer to spend more time with you.

As Daniel Priestley, author of *Key Person of Influence,* said, when people are interested in you they want to spend more time with you. That time may be spent reading your book or watching videos of you speaking or looking at your blogs. Either way, they may want to "gorge" on your content, so having longer form content, such as entire presentations and speeches, is really useful to deepen the relationship a viewer can choose to have with you.

*Interviews*

Either being interviewed or appearing in an interview with other experts in your field can be great for positioning as well as a smart way of opening up and exposing you to another's audience.

On-screen interviews can either be conducted in-person but are more commonly done via Skype or other online communication programmes. The power of using Skype or FaceTime for your interviews is there is hardly any cost involved and the world is your oyster in terms of who you may want to interview or which shows you want to be featured on.

Bear in mind that in some cases all you need to do is ask to get names that are currently bigger than you to be interviewed by you.

After seeing Russell Brunson at a marketing conference in London, I followed up with him after the show and asked if he would be interviewed. I seriously didn't think I'd have a chance and his schedule would be too busy, but he emailed me to say he'd would be very happy to.

I interviewed him on Skype for members of my Advanced Business Growth Facebook group.

**Interview of Russell Brunson**

Make a list of people who you could interview or who you would benefit from being associated with, and reach out to them via email or Messenger and ask if they want to be interviewed. You'll be surprised how willing people are to say "YES".

*Customer stories and testimonials*

Another way to use video is customer stories and testimonials. These are really effective in breaking down a buyer's resistance to you. They're also deeply personal which really connects with the viewer who looks to testimonials to answer objections and also to place them in context.

**Jessen James Inner Circle Testimonial**

*How To Videos*

Youtube has been built on *How To* videos. But that doesn't mean you should ignore these kinds of videos. These are pure demonstration of knowledge. (And it also helps there types of videos are generate a lot of traffic).

You can record a How To video on anything.

Tomatoes anyone?

How To Grow Tomatoes - BEST Secrets on How To Grow Tomatoes

1,891,090 views

**1.8 Million views on this video**

Notice the type of video I DON'T advocate using is the traditional old-fashioned promotional video businesses used to pay thousands of pounds for.

People just don't like watching marketing videos. They like watching and consuming content they are interested in or which promises a clear benefit. You have to give them value and a reason for watching. That's why these work so powerfully.

*Live video*

In the last 12 months, the Live Video phenomenon has really taken hold of Facebook and Youtube - and, before that, via Periscope. The opportunity to broadcast what you are doing live was both a thrilling and scary way of getting exposure to your audience.

What if something awful happened? Or it all went wrong? Or you made a mistake and couldn't go back and re-edit? Well, that's kinda the point.

People are looking more and more for authenticity in the content they consume (again usually asking the question "is this person I'm watching legit?").

When you're forced to put it out there and you're put on the spot to deliver content live to a watching audience, you can't hide. Your expertise needs to shine through.

Live video isn't for everyone and most people will shudder at the thought of being exposed to the world for all to see. However, if you take a chance the rewards are huge. Facebook, in particular, rewards you for recording live video by giving you greater prominence and visibility in others' news feeds.

At Rocket Marketing Hub, I've committed to broadcasting advice on Facebook Live daily. You can see the updates on our Facebook page at:
www.facebook.com/rocketmarketinghub

**Facebook Groups**

A few years ago you could have built your online presence around your Facebook page. Every time you posted, all your readers would be informed of your new content and you would have been hugely visible on the platform. Not any more.

That was a long time ago, now, it seems. The power of the Facebook Page has diminished to such as extent that people really only use them because they need to be seen to be in a decent state in case people check them. With the shift to paid advertising on Facebook, the algorithm has changed to give Facebook Pages less "reach".

What this means is if you had 100 likes on your Facebook Page and you posted an update only a small percentage of the people who liked the page would see it, i.e. less than 10 per cent.

Fortunately, where one opportunity declines another arises and the launch of Facebook Groups proved another great way of sharing content and giving oxygen to your expertise without it costing you a penny.

A Facebook Group can be secret, private or public depending on how much exposure you want and, unlike a Facebook page, when you post in the group EVERYONE who is a member sees it.

This makes Facebook Groups a different opportunity for you than a Facebook Page. You're not just publishing content on a page; you actively have to build a community or tribe around your subject area.

On the face of it, this sounds daunting - and it can be challenging. Yet, it also gives you an opportunity to develop a base of really engaged readers and individuals who may possibly become your customers.

Facebook Groups are essential for your content strategy because they are a place of publication as well as a place to distribute your existing content and drive people to your lead magnets and offers.

To show you how effective Facebook Groups can be, let me use the example of our own group, called Advanced Business Growth.

I built our own Facebook Group to more than 8,000 members (at the time of writing) and now use the group to generate content, sharing content, fill events, make offers and keep my and the business front of mind to everyone involved in Advanced Business Growth.

Firstly, the name is important. Think carefully about what to call your group so it attracts the right kind of people into the group. It has to be centred around your audience.

So, Advanced Business Growth was chosen because it spoke to entrepreneurs who felt they were more sophisticated and were focused on growing their business.

Compare this with if I had chosen a name like Dorking Businesses Forum or Surrey Businesses. You're not qualifying the group membership in the name.

Once, you have a group name and it is set up, the next task is to attract and engage your community. This is done through a mixture of posting content at least one a day and interacting and engaging with the audience.

On the group, we've now sharing over 25 interviews and I've personally broadcast over 100 Facebook Lives as well as share content, blogs and podcast episodes.

JOIN THE GROUP >>> Join the Advanced Business Growth community. Go to Facebook and apply to join here: www.facebook.com/groups/ advancedbusinessgrowth

If you want to know the impact of a Facebook Group can have on your visibility and positioning, let me tell you about another story from one of the first marketing events we put on.

During that event we were discussing Facebook Groups and a member of the audience said he was going to start one in his area of expertise, Mailchimp.

On stage, I called him out and told him to launch the group right away and get people in the room to join to get it going. Although he was very resistant to doing it that quickly and wanted to take his time messing about with cover headers and lining it all up before launch, he got it done with some support from the people in the room.

Fast forward 18 months and that Mailchimp group is now the biggest Facebook group on Mailchimp in the world, and he's positioned as "The" Mailchimp Expert.

Once you have a group using blogs, post, videos and Live Video will also increase engagement and keep you front of mind for your audience.

# STRATEGY #7
# USE THE RIGHT TOOLS TO BUILD YOUR SYSTEM

You are so lucky. You live in a world where…

… You can shoot a video and in less than a minute broadcast it to the rest of the world for NOTHING.

… You can record yourself talking about your area of expertise and upload it to iTunes who will then distribute what you have to say to millions of listeners all across the world in the form of a podcast.

… You can share images of yourself, your work, your customers and your business in seconds with tags that allow other individuals across the world discover you and connect with you as appropriate.

Compare this to what happened before.

If we wanted to broadcast a video promo of our business we would have to hire an expensive production crew, buy broadcast space on one of a few channels for several thousand pounds and wait days or weeks to see the effects of what we did.

If we wanted to reach a newspaper or magazine audience, we would have to pay thousands of pounds for an ad, have it designed and prepared and then, again, wait weeks or even months before it appeared in the publication.

If you wanted others to see images of you, you literally had to send them a physical photograph in a piece of direct mail. Somewhat odd and very costly.

I think you get the picture. There used to be many insurmountable cost and resource barriers to promoting your business. Those barriers don't exist any more. What's more, you can reach an even bigger global audience than you ever have and you don't have to pay a penny to do so.

Yes, newspapers and magazines can still be very effective and the process hasn't changed wildly. But here's what has:

Now, you have NO excuses for getting your message out there.

Really. Zero. You have opportunity piled up at your front door ready for you to take advantage of it. So why aren't you?

Here's what most people do.

They see what shiny new marketing tools and apps others are using on Facebook and instantly experience FOMO (Fear Of Missing Out). They think to themselves, "Well, if everyone else is using this surely I need to be using this to make more money online?" and they pile into it.

You can predict what happens next. They spend hundreds or even thousands of pounds on a product or programme which simply doesn't fit with what they're doing. They're trying to use technology without having a system in place first.

Technology is great, but it will never replace a well thought-out marketing system and a strategy to take a cold lead who is interested in your content through to becoming a paying customer. No technology is going to show you how to do that on your own.

I despair when I meet entrepreneurs, businesses owners and freelancers who have no idea how to generate leads using content or have a way of bringing interested individuals into their marketing funnel... but somehow believe it is a good idea to be spending several hundred pounds each month on a scheduling or marketing programme they still have no idea how to use.

Build the system first and then find the technology to fit the system, not the other way around.

That's what I mean when I talk about using the right tools. And in many cases the right tools are FREE tools. Yes, yes, I know I said I didn't like the word free when it came to finding customers, but in terms of building our marketing system free is your best friend.

There are really powerful free tools on the market you can use while you are building your system and only once you start generating money through your marketing system does it make sense investing real money so you can add other features like automation so you can buy time and freedom (see the next strategy for an explanation of this).

For email, blogging and Facebook you will pay very little or next to nothing to get started. All social media is free to sign up and use - there's no cost barrier whatsoever to using Youtube, Facebook, LinkedIn, Instagram,

Snapchat, twitter, etc for building and growing your audience.

If you're taking payments through credit card transactions, you can even use Paypal to get started and then change to a more powerful transaction provider when you have sales coming in.

There are some exceptions where the right software just isn't free and you will need to invest - though, it really does have to be exponentially worth it to make that change.

There is only one more piece of online software right now that it makes sense to use within your business. It's landing page software called Clickfunnels and will form the basis of all your marketing systems and funnels and simplifies the whole process.

Previous to Clickfunnels building a marketing journey for your customer was a nightmare. You had to create lots of separate web pages and connect these to payment processors and email tools. When Clickfunnels came along it made the creating the entire funnel easier.

It transformed how long it took used to set-up funnels in our business. I saved so much time and money on technical costs of building funnels and could now get an entire funnel up and running within hours rather than days and weeks.

If you've not used Clickfunnels before, you'll soon discover just how easy it is to help you build your first funnel and get it working. If you would like to try Clickfunnels, you can receive a free 14 day trial when you sign up through this link:

http://bit.ly/rocketfunneltrial

The importance thing to remember is the success of your sales and marketing process is nothing to do with technology. Tech is there to make an existing marketing system work better and automate as much of the process as possible so you have greater freedom and independence, as the next section will explain...

# STRATEGY #8
# PAY TO SCALE

EVERYONE on the internet and on Facebook is obsessed with getting traffic for free.

While the Holy Grail of free traffic is possible with some smart SEO and well placed links, you need to start thinking about paying. It's the only way to ensure predictability.

People try to skip to this stage. Buying paid traffic is sexy. Everyone loves the idea of putting £1 into Facebook advertising and hoping to get £10 at the end is the name of the game. Sadly, it doesn't match the reality.

If you go into paid traffic too early in the process, you will lose your shirt (and possibly even more if you get it wrong on places like Google Adwords). But when you're following a marketing system, like the one outlined in this book you'll discover that once you create a system that converts, sending traffic to that offer won't be a risk at all.

It will send your campaigns into orbit and spread your message further and faster than you ever believed.

It's not *really* about paying for advertising. It's about creating a complete system that allows you to gain traffic from multiple sources, including social media, email marketing, videos and podcasts - as well as in-person events and speaking gigs.

Before you even touch paid advertising you need to know your system works and is successful at turning cold leads into customers.

The one skill you need to master when you start building a system like this is knowing your numbers.

Why I love digital marketing so much is because everything is about the numbers. You can track exactly how much you spend on bringing visitors to your website, exactly how many convert and know to-the-penny how much it costs you to acquire a new lead or a new customer.

Thankfully, even if you're not great at numbers it's really simple to understand the fundamentals and make smart decisions based on real data.

If there are two mindset shifts you need to have about paid traffic, to make it work for you, they are:

**Paying for traffic is GOOD.**

It is good for you there's a way of turning the tap of traffic on in your business if you need it.

The reason why some people get burned or cry that Google Adwords or Facebook advertising is "too expensive" or "doesn't work" has nothing to do with paying for traffic. It is because they're using it without thinking about their conversions or ascending their customer up the value ladder. Get these fixed before turning the tap on.

## 2. Buying traffic gives you predictability, not risk

Understanding your numbers will guarantee you don't take risks on advertising that doesn't work. Knowing your numbers and knowing you have a functioning, powerful marketing system working behind your business will deliver everything you need to take your audience from consumers of your content to highly engaged customers who love what you do.

It's not magic, it's marketing. The next strategy will explain the how to finally use a marketing system to win back your time…

# STRATEGY #9
# AUTOMATE FOR INDEPENDENCE

Nearly every online guru or internet marketer will at some point come across or use the following image in a presentation or webinar:

It is the often dreamed-of idea of Nirvana. Having a lifestyle that allows you to run your business from a laptop on the beach in some tropical location where you don't have a care in the world and can sip Pina Coladas all day while staring at your laptop and watching your riches pour into your bank account.

That single image and promise of a laptop beach lifestyle has single-handedly destroyed more businesses and ruined the careers of up-and-coming experts than any recession or single problem with their marketing.

Great businesses who were doing everything right and great coaches who had invested time and effort into building growing expert businesses gave up what was seen as the "hard work" of consistent, valuable content creation and promotion to their audience in favour of the dream.

The dream that NEVER comes true.

That you can make money while you sleep by automating everything in your business. You can automate your Facebook ads. You can automate your follow-up via email and your booking processes. You can automate your customer's purchase process and all your back-end bookkeeping practices. You can even automate the delivery of your programmes.

Hell, you never have to see another client or customer ever again when you have your whole business on autopilot!

It sounds so seductive and appealing. And that's the dangerous part... because it's a complete lie for the 99.9% of businesses who would never benefit from working this way.

It all goes back to the reason why you are building a marketing system in the first place. If you have still to hit your desired income goals or gain the time you want back from your business, the promise of untold riches without having to lift a finger will be a big pull. I get that.

But automation needs to be seen in the context of the wider marketing system and what you are doing to create *real* value in people's lives as well as your own.

Yes, we're going to build automation into your business and the way you market your business. But we're going to do it strategically, in a way that fits with how you position yourself and how you want to be perceived by your ideal customer.

Here are bad reasons for wanting to automate your business:

- You don't have to speak to clients again
- You don't want to do any selling and prefer it to happen when you're not looking
- You can avoid the tough work and instead go on holiday or sit on your sofa at home

Here are very good reasons for adding automating into your business and your marketing systems:

- So you don't miss anything in the follow-up process
- So your readers and customers will get what you said you would deliver, when you said you would deliver it to them
- So you enhance your customer's experience by making it easier to consume your products or services
- So you can create a predictable chain of events which help lead your reader to the sale

Here's the truth:

You CAN'T automate everything.

If you try to take automation too far, it has serious drawbacks. If can very quickly alienate your audience and make them feel like a cog in a bigger machine.

That's often the feedback of many who don't feel special in any way by businesses that put them in a generic email follow-up loop. That's also where you can stand out and gain advantage over other businesses who prefer to automate the important customer touch points.

Here's an example where automation used well can have a big impact. Rather than have your email system automatically send out an email reminder after six months since a customer purchased, you can set up an automation to either get a order placed with a florist to send them a bunch of flowers to thank them for their business or automate a reminder which then triggers the sending of a physical card and a personal message. Think those sound a bit over the top? I know businesses who use exactly these methods to WOW their customers and rocket the number of referrals they receive simply because they've used automation the right way.

Automation is at work here but done in a way so that it adds value to the customer and creates a memorable experience for them. Remember, much of the value you bring is about how you make your customer *feel*.

There's not much more to add than this around automation apart from saying that its execution is the most important thing to get right. It can't and shouldn't be used everywhere. In the following examples, automation done well will help smooth your marketing system and improve your readers', listeners' and viewers' perception of you and your business.

Here's way to get your business working with automation:

- **Webinars** - webinars are still one of the most powerful means to deliver expert information to your target audience in a more engaging and compelling way than generic videos or training. However, they can be highly time-consuming. Now, it is possible to record a webinar and then automated the whole process so that viewers can watch replays or "like-live" versions of the webinar which look like it is being broadcast live but is actually a recording. The reason why "like-live" webinars work well is that the interested individual feels like they'll miss out if they don't attend soon and so there is a much better show-up rate. As well as the webinar itself, it is ideal to automate the whole webinar registration process, reminders and follow-ups. Most webinar software allows you to do this.

- **Emails** - there really is no need for you to personally write and send an email every day. For starters, it is time-consuming and it could take you away from other activities. Email is one of your most powerful marketing tools, so it seems a waste not to automate some of the work to take advantage of email without the hassle. Well, email automation is the answer. Email automation comes in the form of automated sequences (often known as autoresponder sequences). These are usually triggered when a reader downloads a lead magnet or ebook on a subject. An automated email sequence of a few emails are triggered to automatically follow-up with the reader and move them to booking an appointment or buying some kind of offer. Email automation may also be used when a reader comes into your world for the first time. Using a short email sequence for new subscribers allow us to explain our story and how we can help. And of course there is the regular pattern of weekly emails. Rather than sit down once a week to write emails, it makes more sense to dedicate time to creating ALL the emails for the month and automated their publication.

- **Follow-up** - I briefly touched upon the power of follow-up. As the saying goes "the fortune is in the follow-up" meaning that it often takes a long time to turn readers and prospects into paying customers, so constant follow-up is important to keep the sale coming. Doing that manually can involve something as simple as a spreadsheet and enough time to make it work. A better, less manual solution is to use automation for follow up. This may be something as simple as email follow-up emails triggered after a certain amount of time or reminders to give different prospects a call.

# STRATEGY #10
# TAKE MASSIVE ACTION

Success is not a product of intelligence or creativity. We've been led to believe there is some kind of secret to making money that allows you to succeed on a huge scale without needing to do anything.

It's a myth.

Earlier, I discussed the idea of modelling success and following what works. What applies to marketing systems and funnels also applies to people.

The reason I'm showing you a complete marketing system which will take you from where you are now to become a highly sought-after, highly paid authority in your profession is because I know you can do it.

Not that you're special. Look, I don't mean that in a funny way, simply that deciding to be successful is a matter of choice.

It's NOTHING to do with the resources you have available. We've already taking a sword to the myth you need money to get started. There are free tools all around you.

It's NOTHING to do with your ability. If you deliver value to your perfect customer and they love what you do, that's enough. You just need to shine a light on what you do, better.

And now, after reading this it NOTHING to do with your knowledge. This book contains everything you need.

So it comes down to a single choice: Are you ready to take MASSIVE action to get this thing going?

Every high level entrepreneur and leader in their industry shared this trait - the ability to take MASSIVE action.

Every millionaire and multimillionaire I've masterminded or consulted with has this trait - the ability to take MASSIVE action.

It's NEVER about age, ability, knowledge, skills or resources. It is ALWAYS about your implementation.

Will you be an implementor? Or will you keep wishing, hoping and praying for a bigger income?

Will you put what you learned in this book into action, or will you join everyone else who talks the talk and never walks the walk?

Let me reveal a story from a recent Digital Marketing Masterclass I ran.

Now, I've had the full range of people join me on these three day workshops. Everyone from pensioners looking to make more money to top up their savings through to some of the UK's most high profile entrepreneurs.

I've delivered the same fundamental programme with several key tweaks over the last two years - taking into account the huge changes in Facebook and online marketing. What is really interesting is the difference of those who attend, go home and are still stuck and those who attend, put it into action and make an extra £10,000 or £20,000 as a direct result of what they learned.

There's no difference in what is being taught.

There's no difference in the amount of time they have.

There's not even a difference in the resources available (every attendee has full access to video recording equipment and the same technology as everyone else for the duration of the three days).

The only difference is the desire of those who want to be successful to implement immediately and on a huge scale.

They don't drift off at lunchtime to talk on their phone, or head straight for the bar at the end of the day. They're still in the training room, putting everything they learned that day into practice, shooting and re-shooting videos and working at getting it done.

They're the ones who have all the questions the next day. They're the ones who get shit done. And they're the ones who celebrate in a big way within days of finishing the workshop.

Here's what I would love for you to take from this. The successful people I'm talking about aren't special or different. They're no different from you. The only difference is their commitment to act.

Make the same commitment to take MASSIVE action and you will succeed as they do.

Now we've got that out the way, let's move onto our final strategy. And this one will unlock everything when you follow it correctly…

# STRATEGY #11
# USE A PROVEN SYSTEM

There is a popular saying repeated often by Clickfunnels founder Russell Brunson that is relevant to anyone trying to sell themselves online or use Internet marketing to grow their business.

When looking down upon a crowd of wet-behind-the-ears business owners desperate to get started building an online business, he tells them this…

*"Pioneers have arrows in their backs"*

What he means by this is that originality can be very costly. The entrepreneurs and business owners operating in a market for the first time will have taken a huge hit in terms of costs, time and effort in creating a system that works.

Starting an idea from scratch and trying to run with it without any proof it works will cost you in terms of time, money, efforts and the opportunity you have lost.

If you want to build a successful business for your coaching consultancy freelancing or online business, you need to model systems that *already* work. There is no need to reinvent the wheel to build a business of your dreams.

This is what some call "ethically" stealing. However ,I prefer to use the term "success modelling" because that is, essentially, what we are trying to achieve - building out an existing model of a success sales funnel. It simply means looking at what successful people are doing online and following the same process as the starting point for your system.

There are few reasons for this:

- To get your system of the ground quickly and working for you as quickly as possible. Remember taking massive action is key and the quicker you act for better or closer you will come to increasing your income

- You're taking advantage of all the testing and research and cost of failure that other business go through on the road to finding the best way of selling a product or service. You can take advantage of their costly mistakes by modelling their system and using that as the basis for your own.

- The market moves quickly. If you take ages to set up and test a system, your customers may already have moved on. This gives you current market access, quickly

Note that I say "starting point" in relation to the activity suggested. Every business starts with one system at the start and most of the time it doesn't work perfectly, if at all. Just think back to when you first started your business. Did you have a system for making sales or producing marketing that worked? Probably not. It developed as time rolled by and was gradually improved upon and changed until it looks like the process you have now.

**The perfect marketing system for you**

When I started out on digital marketing I made a whole load of mistakes. I threw thousands of pounds down the drain, wasted hours and hours on marketing that didn't work and paid the price in lost opportunities.

Now, having built and run digital marketing campaigns for hundreds of businesses - including some of the biggest companies in the UK - there are some principles I know now that I wished someone had told me when I started my agency after my accessories business folded.

The mistake nearly every business makes is seeing digital marketing in its isolated parts. For example, their marketing will consist of a single part. They will be running a Facebook ad or they will be posting on social media and see that as a whole marketing strategy. It isn't. A marketing SYSTEM needs to consist of multiple elements working together that results in what you ultimately want: sales.

If sales isn't the main driver of your marketing system, there's no point in doing it. I hear so many business owners talk about awareness and branding and social media "reach". Those are all great as SECONDARY aims of your marketing. Sales should always be the first goal of marketing. The success of a campaign can only truly be measured in pounds and pence and how much profit it added to your business.

**Why you need a system**

In business, it helps to have a system; in fact, it helps to have THE SYSTEM.

All of the major names in business have developed their own marketing system and use this as the template for their business.

Even though they have issues and troubles to overcome, major firms like McDonald's and Tesco are successful because they have systems that they know work, and they follow that system day-in, day-out to bring in new customers, make sales and increase profits.

Here's the thing. Don't be fooled into thinking that only big firms can benefit from working this way. It can be of great benefit to start-ups and companies being led by one or two people. It can also work whether you sell products, services or even digital products. In fact, all your marketing should work within a system otherwise you are most likely losing money and wasting effort.

Before we go on, let's first define some key business principles which will inform what we need from our marketing system.

According to business guru Jay Abraham, there are fundamental elements of business growth that apply to EVERY business whether you're a one-person coaching business or a multibillion pound corporate. The fact is this - there are only three ways to grow your business:

1. By increasing the NUMBER OF CUSTOMERS that you have

2. By increasing the AVERAGE TRANSACTION VALUE for every customer

3. By increasing the NUMBER OF TRANSACTIONS for every customer

Any system you use for marketing needs to work to do all three of these things on a consistent basis to keep your business moving forward.

In my businesses and with my clients, I teach a marketing system I've developed over many years having successfully helped thousands of businesses increase sales and grow. It's the same system that has helped me sell more goods worth more than £20 million in value. And it's the same system I show to new, up-and-coming businesses to quickly move from stuck and not earning enough to creating a constant stream of high value leads and sales.

As an expert, this system is perfectly set up for you and will give you all the elements needed to quickly position yourself as the best-known in your field, attract the attention of the right customers and move them quickly to spending money with you.

When you learn this, you'll kick yourself for its simplicity and how much it makes sense. However, you won't learn any of this from a marketing degree or from a business school. Unlike many of the so-called online marketing gurus who try selling you their unproven system, this exact system was forged from hard-won experience in selling services and thousands of products, both physical and digital, in the real world.

**Expert Mastery Income System**

The system I'll show you today is called the Expert Mastery Income System and is designed to achieve several goals. These are:

- Attracting the attention of the right buyers

- Capturing their details with some kind of exchange mechanism
- Make a valuable offer to persuade them to spend money with you and become a customer
- Try selling them a higher value product
- Keep them engaged and offer them further opportunities to buy relevant products or services with you

Taken as a whole, this system hits all three principles outlined by Jay Abraham in driving business growth.

Here are how they steps of the business university look:

When you build this system in your business, you will find results come quicker than you can imagine. It's my aim to give you everything you need in these pages so you can implement this right away and start enjoying results.

To help you do that, let's go through each element in the system and I'll explain how it fits with the 11 strategies of Expert Mastery to win over your prospect, turn them into a customer and help you reach your income goals.

Let's get started

**Content Phase (#1) - The Expert Content**

The first phase of the system is developing Expert Content. As outlined in the earlier Expert Mastery strategies, the purpose of the early stages of your customer's experience is consuming content you have produced. This phase is all about creating the right type of content to put in front of the right audience at the right time.

This content phase is a mix of blogging, video content, Facebook activity and using ways to bring your perfect audience together in a way that allows you to control the conversation while constantly serving them with your advice and value.

Using a detailed customer avatar, the plan during this phase is to work on achieving the three key parts of the success formula:

- Position yourself as the "go-to" expert in your field

- Increase your presence from "invisible" to "highly visible" thus reinforcing your positioning in the market

- Doing this on a consistent and predictable basis so your audience can rely and anticipate your knowledge, thereby increasing their desire to continue following you

To achieve this during this phase, you develop a plan for your content production and distribution that maximises the impact of every piece of content you create. For example, you may create a single video then use it to create several other pieces of content that can them be published in different places - for example as a blog post and as a Facebook update.

You may record a podcast interview with someone with a large audience who is your target market. It may be possible to repurpose that very interview to create a written blog post, an audio post, a series of social media updates, a video interview for use on Youtube, Facebook and LinkedIn, a LinkedIn update and even a series of shorter audio clips and soundbites for distribution on social media channels.

As you can see the focus is working on smarter, not necessarily harder, and making every piece of content production sweat to produce results for you. During this phase it's all about planning what needs to be done to make you as visible as possible in the shortest space of time and doing that on a consistent basis to build your positioning.

## Capture Phase (#2) - The Stress Free Lead Generator

The next phase of the system revolves around an important step and the important first act of trust they will have with you - sharing their personal details.

The first step of building any relationship is when your prospective customer gives you their personal contact details - in the form of their email address or mobile number - to implicitly give you permission to contact them again.

The purpose of this phase is to create assets and find reasons for them to give you those details in the first place. What can you create or give that would prove so valuable to your prospective customer they would hand over their personal details without thinking twice.

That's why in this phase we're focused on the lead magnet and building the first part of the marketing system to lead the reader from content to lead magnet download so we capture their details and get them on the database and email list ready for the next stages.

Getting them on the list is the most important step of the whole process. Why? Because once they are on the list, ANY communication to them is free. You have direct access to their inbox and it makes it much easier to sell and promote your products as well as get them to consume your content when you have their email address.

What makes this phase simpler than most other system is our Stress Free lead generation method where I work with businesses to go through a formula and system that makes this easy work. Too many experts and business get hung up on lead magnets and downloadable content.

They spent hours and hours crafting the perfect lead magnet, only to discover no-one actually wants it. When you do this right you'll know before you even start putting it together whether your audience actually wants it, saving you time, money and effort.

**Customer Phase (#3) - The Micro Purchase Solution**

Looking back at the Expert Mastery strategy on the value ladder, you know by now that the next most important step for a potential customer is actually BECOMING A CUSTOMER. And that's where the Micro Purchase solution comes in. It is a step designed to transform a reader into a customer by engineering a transaction between the two.

In this phase, your aim is to develop a high-value but ridiculously low-ticket offer that makes the purchase almost impossible to refuse.

If you have your audience's pain points and challenges nailed and you really know what they're looking for help with, you can very easily develop a solution which moves them some way towards solving their problem without "giving away the farm".

If you can understand this step and get it right, you will find yourself ahead of your rivals and competitors. The number one aim at this step to increase the number of customers that you have and the use of the lead magnet has generated leads, but it hasn't delivered new customers yet.

The Micro Purchase is aimed at those who have shown an interest via the lead magnet. Your Micro Purchase should usually be an irresistible offer available at a super low price (offering deals for £1/$1 or up to a reasonable value exist to solely bring people on-board and convert the prospects into buyers). Obviously, the cost of the offer should be relative to the overall cost of your product or service and high cost products can have successful Micro Purchase offers at a high price, just make sure that it is relevant.

You have to make an offer that is impossible to resist or turn down. A very common way of doing this is to sell your offering at cost, or even at a loss. You will not be able to make a living from your Micro Purchase offering, but you will be able to acquire buyers, and this is where the real value comes in. There are few things, if any, in business that are more valuable than having access to a list of buyers.

When you understand this system, you understand how vital the Micro Purchase offer is and how important it is to your business, even if you are unable to make a profit from the offer.

This isn't anything new, by the way. Here are some great examples of Micro Purchases.

Readers of a certain vintage will remember in the 1980s and 90s that a number of music labels and companies would provide buyers the chance to buy a collection of albums (be it on vinyl, tape or CD) for a low price. There were some offers that provided people with 12 CD albums for £1!

## Columbia House Micro Purchase

This was a deal that people signed up to in droves to save money and while it sounds like a big loss-maker to the company, the benefit of acquiring a list of buyers was the biggest aspect for them.

You can carry out Micro Purchase offerings with physical products, books, software, paid webinars or even services, just like Groupon does.

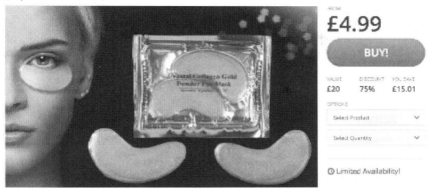

40 Collagen Eye Masks or 5 Collagen Face Masks from £4.99 (Up to 75% Off)

**£4.99**

BUY!

| VALUE | DISCOUNT | YOU SAVE |
|---|---|---|
| £20 | 75% | £15.01 |

OPTIONS

Select Product

Select Quantity

⏱ Limited Availability!

**Groupon is full of micro purchases.**

Micro purchases are a very common part of business and they are all around us. You may have heard that Amazon sells Kindles at a low price, and this is true, and it is a great example of this in action.

Even if Amazon makes a loss on every Kindle they sell, when people buy books or apps to place on that Kindle, Amazon makes the sale. You will find it with companies who are on Groupon or any other coupon based company. You may think that getting £50 worth of food for £20 is a great deal for you, but it is also a great deal for the company because they can then reach out to you directly.

## Amazon Kindle is a loss leader.

You should look to convert the highest possible number of lead magnet leads into customers that pay, even if you impact your profit margin. You should do this because if you acquire a paying customer, your will obtain a profit through the next few steps.

This is a really important step. Get this wrong and nothing from this point works, which considering it is all transaction-based and mainly profit after the Micro Purchase point, would be a disaster for your marketing system.

Because once they've made a micro purchase, it's time to serve them with…

## Core Offer Phase (#4) - The Profitable Product Blueprint

This is where you make your money: on the core offer. Knowing how to structure your core offer and when to present it to your audience in the right way is what this phase deals with.

You should already have a core offer in place, it should be your flagship product or service. A lot of businesses try to sell their core offers directly to cold prospects, but they find that this gets them nowhere. However, if you are able to make your core offer after a lead magnet and Micro Purchase offer, you should find that your sales increase greatly.

This makes sense because you have already had two successful transactions with the buyer and it is vital that you over-deliver on these offerings.

It is possible to make enough sales, or the right sales, from your core offer that you become profitable but you don't need to, and it can be difficult to achieve. When it comes to using this system correctly, many businesses take everything they receive from the core offer and then reinvest it to pick up more customers. This is the way to build a business and if you do it right, you can achieve great success.

It is possible to create a system where you spend more than your rivals when it comes to acquiring customers. With so many businesses trying to make their profits from a core offer, think about how strong you will be if you don't have to make a penny of profit from your core offer?

Jeff Bezos from Amazon stated about business rivals: "Your margin is my opportunity."

You have an opportunity to spend more on acquiring traffic, on converting and increasing the value of what you offer.

Here's something else I've found.

One things I invariably find when working with entrepreneurs and experts. They don't know what their core offer is… and that's completely normal. They may have been working on the basis of an hourly rate or a daily rate. They may have completed ad hoc projects for specific clients. They may have no system for what they charge.

Well, this phase gets you to focus on what your core offer could be and for many of my students it's at this stage it becomes transformative for them. When you create a business around a proven marketing system you begin to see opportunity for leverage and building an offer which can actually free you from the constraints of hourly rates and marching to the beat of your customers' tune all the time.

The core offer needs to be highly valuable and it's effectiveness proved beyond all doubt. At this stage the customer should be highly aware of who you are, how you can help and what the big promise of the product is. This is where hiring marketing professionals really helps in defining and selling your profitable product. A good sales copywriter will help pull out the features and benefits and find an angle to sell your core offer with.

With this in mind, will it shock you to learn that a great number of hugely successful businesses do not make any profit until the reach the following two stages? This is where the process becomes very interesting.

## Continue Phase (#5) - The Ethical Upserve Solution

The second stage of the business growth model cited by Jay Abraham is to increase the average transaction value for every customer and this is what this Upserve Solution achieves.

You will find that many businesses do not have a Micro Purchase offer, nor do they have an Upserve Solution. They try to solely live on their core offer, and sell this by reaching out to cold prospects. This is why these firms struggle and why, if you follow this marketing system, you won't.

A great example of how to do things right can be seen with McDonald's.

The global burger chain makes virtually no money on their hamburger, which is their core offer. However, when they offer their Upserve Solution - or profit maximiser, as it is sometimes known - of fries and a soft drink - and the customer buys - the profits soar.

This is referred to as an "immediate up-sell" and they are not the only company that performs in this manner. If you have ever bought an electrical appliance or white goods at a great price, were you then offered a warranty, installation support or assistance? These are Upserve solutions.

Once someone becomes a customer and has taken your core offer, now you have the opportunity few businesses enjoy. Making almost maximum profit on any promotions to your customers going forward (if these are digital products, of course).

Many things can go wrong at this stage because businesses abuse the trust they spent so much time building up and feel this is now the opportunity to bombard that customer with as many offers and promotions as possible in the hope they will be hammered into submission and buy more. Something, ANYTHING.

Just because they have bought your core offer once, doesn't mean your audience is now interested in any and every offer you have.

That's why we focus on the *Ethical* Upserve - that means putting the right offers in front of customers to maximise profits but ultimately help them keep moving forward in a targeted, non-intrusive and ethical way.

This is where this system works so much better than others out there and succeeds in building real long-term value for your brand or business, which

means streams of happy customers who are only too happy to provide you with incredible testimonials and case studies and referrals.

This is hugely important. Like I mentioned earlier, on the strategy about selling more by selling less, we're not going to bombard with offers. We'll only put offers to our market when they raise their hand to say they are interested in something.

For example, once we have captured their data they will automatically go into an automated email sequence that sends them a few important welcome emails to introduce who I am and who we are, as a business. This short series is designed to move them from knowing not a lot about our business to understand exactly why we do what we do and how we may be able to help them in the future.

They are then put onto our main list to receive engagement emails and advice every week. Within that content there is an opportunity to go into different topics in more detail, with the reader signifying their interests by click to download items or discover more.

The highest level of expense for a company is the cost of acquiring the customer, which your Micro Purchase should take care of, and then after this point, everything can play a role in increasing the immediate and lifetime value of a customer.

To get started on this, you should think about:

- What could you offer as a cross-sell or an up-sell?
- Is there anything you can bundle together with your core offer?
- Can you incorporate a membership or subscription service to your business model?

When you find your Ethical Upserve Solutions, your business will become unstoppable. And with the final step, you'll make sure you never leave any money on the table.

## Bringing them back with a return path

The final way to grow your business is to increase the number of transactions you have with a customer and this is why setting up a "return path" makes sense.

The aim of this return path is to develop frequent and strategic communication with prospects and buyers that will ensure they buy from you on a regular basis. You have contact information for these people, obtained through the lead magnet, and this means that you have the ability to reach out to these customers time and time again.

It is possible to offer new lead magnets, new Micro Purchase offers, new Core Offers and new Ethical Upserves because you have people's permission. You can even take them back to any offer they didn't buy the first time.

This return path plays a vital role in bringing your customer or prospect back to you on a regular basis and it can include retargeting, social media, sales call, content marketing or automated email sequences.

**Putting the system together**

Once you have all the phases of the Expert Mastery Income System in place, there are other elements to add to it, such as running traffic to content and adding in elements such as remarketing and retargeting to bring people right back into the offer cycle.

However, this is the most powerful starting point.

Now, standing back looking from where you began, I've shown you what you need to become a highly paid expert, how to use the strategies of Expert Mastery to position yourself perfectly for your audience, increase your presence everywhere consistently and use digital marketing to create a system that moves people who don't know you to becoming customers in a very short space of time.

Yes, it's a lot. And as I sit here writing it feels as though I've given away a lot (almost too much), but this is what

I teach and so I'm pleased if it helps you go forward and build a valuable business that helps others, too.

# WHAT TO DO NEXT

Ok, ok, you've just been hit with a huge amount of information. By reading this book, you'll have gained all the knowledge to go from whatever place you are now to becoming the expert in your field. You now know how to position yourself as an expert, use the right tools to gain the awareness of your target market and take them on a journey to becoming your customer.

That's a lot to take on in one time and I recommend you read through this book another two or three times to fully get every lesson and strategy I've written about.

But, it certainly wouldn't surprise me if, after reading this book, you're probably left thinking:

*"There's just so much to do, where do I start?"*

Don't panic. Breathe deeply. I'm going to show you exactly where to start so you can finally raise your income, break free from the limitations holding you back and gain the independence and financial freedom you really want.

Even though it seems like a lot to take in, the basic process really isn't that complicated. You just need to follow the steps laid out in this book and I guarantee you'll get to where you want to go. I know this because this is the exact process I used for my own businesses and the exact process I've taken thousands of students through, many of whom have gone on to be hugely successful, well-paid and recognised experts.

**Here's what you need to do next**

If you haven't gone back through this book, make that your No.1 priority and this time use a notepad or open a Word document while you're reading it. But don't just make notes, make these ACTION POINTS.

As I wrote earlier in the book, knowing all this is useless. Completely and utterly useless... unless you take MASSIVE action to get these points implemented as soon as possible.

Sure, you may not fully understand how to use some of the technology and processes I've mentioned along the way, but there are things you CAN do right now to get started. And getting started is the hardest part.

So DO it.

Want to know the best first step? Start sharing your value RIGHT NOW. Like right this minute. Put this book down, get on Facebook or open up the camera on your phone and shoot a 90 second video giving your audience your best piece of advice. Answer a frequently asked question or share something about your working day. It doesn't have to be perfect first time.

Get something out there and let it start working. Don't worry about how you'll come across - your expertise and experience will shine through.

Then, if you're serious about becoming the success you always wanted to be, the next thing you should do is plan your time. Plan the specific days in your week when you will work on getting the steps in this book done. Pull your diary out or open your calendar on your laptop or phone and make an appointment with yourself on a daily or weekly basis to work on THIS.

If you're unsure where to start on building your system, start right at the beginning by looking again at your Customer Avatar. Download the Customer Avatar template, I've provided you right here >>>

www.rocketmarketinghub.com/craft_the_perfect_customer_avatar/

This is the most important thing you should be doing in your life right now - building the income, career and life you really want. Even if you're still in a full time job, or working with clients who take up most of your week or have other commitments, dedicated as little as 10-15 minutes a day will start bringing you results very quickly.

Here's the thing. Most people who read this book WON'T do that. They won't dedicate time to creating the life they want. They won't believe it is possible. They'll read this book, think "that's great" or "that's too good to be true", put this book down and go on with their life.

You don't have to make that *your* choice. You can do it.

So, do it RIGHT NOW.

# AN EXCLUSIVE OFFER FOR EXPERT MASTERY READERS

## I want to help your business grow… for just £1

Hi I'm James Nicholson and I am the founder of Rocket Marketing Hub. I understand that when you think about Digital Marketing, if you're like most businesses, you have no idea where to start. That was my reason for starting Rocket Marketing Hub.

I give you step by step instructions on how to implement the best marketing pillars into your business. Unlike many of the internet marketing "experts" plastered all over your Facebook feed, we're not just a training company - we actually do this stuff day-in, day-out for our own customers at Digital Marketing Desk. I show you what's working right now.

At Rocket Marketing Hub, we know EVERY business is different. We give you step-by-step guides to ROCKET your business to the next level.

For £59 per month, you receive:

- Masterplans – Our set by step tutorials showing you how to implement things like SEO, Facebook Advertising, Google Adwords and more

- Fast Track – Helps you get the basics sorted quickly, get listed in Google for FREE, how to get online reviews and much more

- Webinars – We bring the leading experts in the Digital Marketing World into your world. Watch a full ARCHIVE of webinars at a time to suit you.

- Rocket TV – Every week we bring you bite sized tips and tricks you can implement into your business.

"Rocket Marketing Hub have some amazing ideas that will help grow your business. I love how easy the Master Plans are to follow, simple step by step instructions. I am very busy working in my business that I find it great to do these in bite sized chunks." Charlie Lloyd – lloydhrconsultancy.co.uk

Get your £1 14-day trial with Rocket Marketing Hub and start generating more leads and more sales to help your company achieve LIFT OFF!

www.rocketmarketinghub.com/join_now/

# APPENDIX I - 50 CONTENT IDEAS FOR IMMEDIATE INSPIRATION

While you know the benefits that come from creating regular blog content, it can sometimes be difficult to know what to write about. Coming up with great and relevant ideas can be difficult but if you are looking to engage your audience and promote your business in the most effective and appropriate way, you need to come up with great ideas.

So what do you when inspiration isn't striking? What you need is a GO TO list that will help you to think about brilliant ideas on the spot. If you want to banish writer's block for good, here are 50 ways for you to dream up new content for our blogs, videos and social posts in a second.

1. Ask fellow business owners for a guest post
2. Ask fellow business owners if they will be interviewed
3. Ask other business owners for ideas
4. Ask yourself – what is the biggest issue in my industry? Find the answer for yourself and then share your thoughts or the solution
5. Be analytical – look at what topics have generated most traffic or interest in your site and use this as your starting point for new content
6. Choose a book that your audience will have an interest in and look through the topics for inspiration

7. Create a survey or poll and share it on social media – the poll should ask your users what content they want covered or what issues they need answering

8. Create blog posts that compile your previous blogs into handy reference and resource lists – for instance, if you have written blogs providing resources for Twitter marketing – create a new blog that discusses the topic and then list all of the relevant blogs

9. Find a list post relevant to your business or industry and then expand on any (or all) of the points

10. Get a pen and some paper and "brainstorm" ideas

11. Get yourself over to Reddit and look at what topics are trending – choose a relevant trending topic as your starting point

12. Go for a walk and see if your wander provides you with inspiration

13. Go to a forum for your business, industry or area and read the comments

14. Go to a rival blog and see what is most popular – then give your own slant or opinion

15. Go to www.blogengage.com and consider what relevant writers are discussing

16. Go to www.buzzsumo.com and find out what the most relevant content in your industry is

17. Go to Facebook and check out your news-feed to see what topics are trending

18. Go to Facebook and see if anyone has posted on your page with a question you can answer or a topic you can discuss

19. Go to Facebook and utilise Facebook Interests to create a list of content that is relevant to your industry

20. Go to Facebook or Twitter and engage your audience – the best way to find out what people want to read about is to ask them what they want to read about

21. Go to Facebook or Twitter and listen in on conversations taking place between your followers or people in your area – if there are topics of interest, write about these popular topics

22. Go to Facebook, join a relevant group and see what the relevant topics are

23. Go to Google and search on the keywords you want to rank for – look at the articles being written for this keyword(s) and give your own slant or opinion

24. Go to Google and use the auto-complete function to see what it provides you with

25. Go to Google Keywords Planner and search for relevant keywords in your industry, business or area

26. Go to Instagram and see if relevant pictures provide you with inspiration

27. Go to HubSpot and use their Blog Topic Generator

28. Go to LinkedIn and visit groups that are relevant to your industry and then see what topics are being discussed

29. Go to www.mindthebook.com and see if there are any questions or content that will give you ideas

30. Go to Pinterest and look in popular searches

31. Go to Quora and look for questions that you can answer

32. Go to Stumble Upon and then "stumble upon" topics you want to write about

33. Go to Twitter and check what is trending in the sidebar

34. Go to www.ubersuggest.org and look for suggestions or keywords on a specific topics

35. Go to Yahoo Answers, find questions people want answered and then give an expansive response

36. Go to your blog and read the comments, are people asking questions or commenting on certain topics? If there are, this should be an idea to write about

37. Go to your email analytics and see if there is a topic or headline that gets answered most – if there is, this is what people want to read about

38. Install a plugin like CommentLuv on your WordPress blog to see what your commenters blog about

39. Look at the news and see what is happening

40. Look at your rivals or popular blogs in your niche – are there topics that are popular and that you

have an opinion on? Be original but you can find great inspiration by looking at relevant content

41. Make sure you have Google Alerts set up to provide you with keywords and relevant stories for your business, industry or niche

42. Read an industry magazine and see if anything inspires you

43. Review your offline materials and publications for ideas

44. Search social media for relevant and trending hashtags

45. Showcase different uses for your products or services

46. Spotlight your employees and create a blog post about their average day

47. Think about a question or issue that has always had you stumped and then find the answer – then write about it

48. Through Google, check out Google Trends and see what topics are popular

49. Use the Keyword Niche Finder tool from WordStream to find the most relevant subtopics in your area or niche

50. What question are you most frequently asked by customers? If there are questions that people always ask, answer them

Printed in Great Britain
by Amazon

45828459R00090